CHAMPIONS

Gabe Jaramillo is a Colombian–American tennis coach, entrepreneur, innovator, consultant, writer, influencer and motivational speaker. Jaramillo is senior executive vice president and director of tennis coaching at Altitude International Holdings Inc. and a member of its board of directors. A US-based father of three, he has worked with and developed many of the greatest players in tennis history, including coaching 11 world No. 1s and 27 top 10 players, such as Andre Agassi, Jim Courier, Mary Pierce, Maria Sharapova, Monica Seles and Kei Nishikori. He is also the co-founder of Club Med Academies, now Atlitude Academies. Jaramillo's YouTube channel Tennis On Demand (@ tennisondemand) has more than 50,000 subscribers. He has 105,000 and 137,000 followers on Facebook and Instagram (@gabejaramillocoach), respectively. His website is https://gabejaramillo.com/. His first book, *El Manual Secreto del Tenis*, is a compendium of his methodology.

Gyasi Hall is an essayist and poet born in Columbus, Ohio. His work has appeared in the music project 68to05 (https://www.68to05.com), the art book portal Thoughtcrime Press and various literary journals such as *Black Warrior Review* and *Brink*, among others. His first book of poetry, *Flight of the Mothman: An Autobiography*, in which he explores his own experiences with race and mythology, was published in 2019.

'Parents play a crucial role in supporting and nurturing the development of their children into successful athletes and lifelong champions. In *How to Make Champions*, Gabe Jaramillo reveals his valuable insights into how successful parents can have a dramatic effect on their child's development. Gabe's vast experience working with athletes and their parents from throughout the world gives him unique expertise on how to teach parents the secrets to help build their children into successful athletes and lifelong champions.'

—**Nick Bollettieri**
Tennis coach and International
Tennis Hall of Fame inductee, 2014

'*How to Make Champions* is a unique book guiding parents who are raising elite athletes. High-performance athletes depend on relationships, and there is no one more important than that relationship they have with their parents, especially at an early age. The book is an easy read but get ready to take many notes.'

—**Susan Fields**
Vice President of Product Merchandising, Disney

'*How to Make Champions* is an important read for parents raising elite athletes. High-performance athletes will likely have many coaches but a successful parent–child relationship is a vital ingredient. In this book, Gabe gives the reader key insights to navigate the challenges ahead.'

—**Jim Courier**
Former world No. 1 tennis player and International
Tennis Hall of Fame inductee, 2005

'*How to Make Champions* is a book for every parent that has children playing sports. In it, Gabe shares with all of us his lifelong experience working with world-class athletes, navigating some very challenging dynamics between parent–children relationships. It gives parents the tools to help children reach their highest potential in sports and life. It's a win–win combination. *How to Make Champions* will be a book that, after you read it, you will keep going back to it at different times during the development of your child's athletic career. The book will be a staple in the bag of a serious athlete.'

—Monica Seles
Former world No.1 tennis player and International
Tennis Hall of Fame inductee, 2009

'A parent's job is not to be a child's friend. It's to be the coach. In *How to Make Champions*, Gabe Jaramillo explains how parents' and coaches' function is to provide an environment and age-appropriate challenges that will allow a young person to develop the skills, habits and values they'll need to become independent, strong, honest and trustworthy adults. *How to Make Champions* provides a jump start and a plan easy to navigate for parents of aspiring athletes.'

—David Fish
Tennis Association Hall of Fame Inductee, 2019

'I've known Gabe for over 10 years, and I am always inspired by his vision and expertise on peak performance. This book is a must-have for parents and athletes who are looking for a winning advantage, not only in sport—but in life!

It takes a team to build a champion, and these practical, actionable insights will prove [to be] an important part of any team.'

—Xavier Mufraggi
President, Young President's Organization

'In *How to Make Champions*, Gabe Jaramillo draws on his long and extraordinary career as a coach to illustrate very valuable concepts for those who aspire to be elite athletes. A must-have book for parents, coaches and athletes, spiced up with dozens of interesting anecdotes from many of the tennis players Gabe helped rise to the top, and a fantastic guide for those looking to be champions on and off the court.'

—**José Pablo Coello**
Reporter and anchor, Fox Sports

'Becoming a champion is not an accident and involves parents playing a critical role in developing and nurturing talent. Gabe Jaramillo is a rare expert who understands what it takes for young athletes to achieve extraordinary results. In *How to Make Champions*, he shares the unique expertise he has built, through decades of elite athlete development, so that parents can help their children fully maximize their potential.'

—**Kumar Mehta**
Author of *The Exceptionals: How the Best Become the Best and How You Can Too* and the bestselling *The Innovation Biome*

'I would like to emphasize the importance of investing more and more in the education and preparation of parents. However, we need to be aware that while investing time in developing players, it is also essential to work with parents. I believe Gabe Jaramillo has had rich experience with parents throughout his career. This book will help coaches train parents to be better prepared to help their children reach their maximum potential.'

—**Cesar Kist**
Developmental officer,
International Tennis Federation

HOW TO MAKE
CHAMPIONS

FROM THE GROUND UP: RAISING CHAMPIONS
FOR LIFE THROUGH SPORTS

GABE JARAMILLO
GYASI HALL

RUPA

Published by
Rupa Publications India Pvt. Ltd 2023
7/16, Ansari Road, Daryaganj
New Delhi 110002

Sales centres:
Prayagraj Bengaluru Chennai
Hyderabad Jaipur Kathmandu
Kolkata Mumbai

P-ISBN: 978-93-5702-228-6
E-ISBN: 978-93-5702-223-1

First impression 2023

10 9 8 7 6 5 4 3 2 1

The moral right of the authors has been asserted.

Printed in India

While writing this book, I went back to my childhood, to those afternoons of long conversations with my mother sitting in wicker and pine rocking chairs on the balcony of my grandmother's house. The waves crashed nonchalantly against the rocks and the sea breeze caressed our cheeks. 'My love, we live for our children, we work for our young athletes but they don't belong to us,' she would say to me. They were wise words, moments full of teachings. Yet, I always felt her soul was heavy. 'In the blink of an eye, everything will be useless. Many will triumph but others will drift without a compass or escort. They will be the masters of our sleepless nights.' In my mother's despondent heart, there always remained many doubts. What anguished helplessness. Only now do I feel the weight and responsibility of our accepted destiny. How right you were, my mother. They are borrowed. Every phrase and teaching I wrote in this book and all my accomplishments are deeply rooted in conversations, stories and dialogues with Fanny, my mentor and inspiration. This book is for her.

CONTENTS

Preface: Why This Book?   *xi*

Section I
How to Get Started as an Athlete

1. Talent   3
2. Early Specialization   16
3. Sequence and Spheres   25

Section II
Fundamentals

4. Planning   35
5. Volume   42
6. Quality   50
7. Repetition   57

Section III
Training Nuances

8. Variation   65
9. Specificity   72
10. Competition   76
11. Knowledge   87
12. Communication   95
13. Male and Female Athletes   104
14. Individuality   116

Section IV
The Mental Part

15. Imagination   127
16. Fearless   134
17. Attitude   142
18. Routines   150

Section V
A Player's Support System

19. Parents   161
20. Coaching   177
21. Team and Environment   186
22. Sponsors   195
23. Marketing   204
24. Results   212

Epilogue: Advice from Various Experts   215
Further Reading   231

PREFACE: WHY THIS BOOK?

Let's use sports to achieve happiness, independence and well-being for our children.

There is, undoubtedly, a special sort of transcendent beauty to sports. This is doubly true of elite athletes in particular, the people whose graceful and godlike feats redefine, time and again, what we consider to be humanly possible. The grace of these accomplishments reinforces the distance between the performer and the spectator. It is a beauty that works on every level; a spectacle that does not need a certain amount of skill or ability to be understood. Whether you're a fan, a player yourself or even a total novice, there is much to be idolized about athletes, much to be broken down about their playing and much to be understood about the depth and invariable ungodliness of their commitment.

We all understand, through myth, marketing and physical self-evidence, what the results of these players' journeys are but what we do not really grasp are the nuances of what it takes to get there. This is due in large part to those same engines of legendary status; the forces that create these athletes and allow them to thrive can also clash with the end product—an unpleasant reality that can undermine the awesome and almighty image of the athletes themselves. Simply put, training schedules, mental exercises, coaching techniques and tournament planning only appeal to a mass audience when these things bolster the player's exceptionalism and their other-worldliness. Anything beyond that becomes boring and seemingly inconsequential.

Of course, those of us who are really steeped in this industry know that it is this part of the journey, the road and not where it leads, so to speak, that is not only the most vital but the most interesting part of the whole process. We know that truly great elite athletes are not born from the results of any one match or tournament or out of the hype of unbelievable highlights and good press but, rather, out of years of intense training and conditioning well before glory.

This book has been written to help parents and coaches navigate these parts of an elite athlete's career and to offer a comprehensive outline to arrive at the top level of gameplay through both practical physical steps as well as training philosophy to help build a true competitor's mindset. This book is designed to peel back and examine all the variables that go into fostering elite athleticism and the ways in which these variables intersect and interact. This book tackles these relationships from a variety of angles in order to get at the heart of what this kind of practice truly involves—stats and stories, studies and research, personal testimony and industry information too often made opaque. Those of us who are true professionals of this field understand how complete and holistic the process of making champions actually is. I have read many coaching books that fail to understand the depth of their own responsibility, to their players and the sport at large. You cannot achieve the sort of greatness we all strive for solely with platitudes or gut instinct or gimmicks or number-crunching; the sort of greatness that we all strive for is much more complicated and demands so much more from us. This book will provide an insight into the depth of that demand and what it takes to meet it.

There are some things to consider: Firstly, what exactly does it mean when I talk about 'elite athletes'? I am talking not only about the athletes that are some of, if not the, best in the history of their respective games but also about those players that seem to have transcended these games altogether—athletes who have become household names and changed their sports forever—Andre Agassi, Serena Williams, Roger Federer and Monica Seles in the world of tennis, and Michael Jordan, Tiger Woods, Michael Phelps and Muhammad Ali outside of it. While many people, between these competitors' other-worldly images and the public's general ignorance of the gritty nature of sports training, tend to view these athletes and their accomplishments as more divine than anything else, which is, as we have established, untrue. The reality of these people and their achievements has less to do with innate talent than with how and when that talent is honed. This relationship between natural ability, how that ability is shaped and how to encourage that relationship in a productive way is a big part of what this book is about.

Secondly, this book will focus primarily on tennis, since that is where the majority of my nearly four decades as a coach and mentor to various world-class athletes have been focussed. However, many of these principles are steeped in various fundamental truths about how to live your life to its fullest potential—guidance based on work ethic, resilience, honesty and honing a healthy competitive spirit. While the minute details may not be universal, the vast majority of these lessons can be applied not just to different sports but also to a large array of other disciplines as well.

On 9 July 2011, Andre Agassi was inducted into the International Tennis Hall of Fame. During his acceptance speech, he reflected on the power of tennis as a tool of self-actualization beyond the court:

> It's no accident that tennis uses the language of life. Service. Advantage. Break. Fault. Love. The lessons of tennis are the lessons of maturity... Tennis teaches you the subtlety of human interaction, the curse and blessing of cause and effect. When you play tennis for a living, you never forget that we are all connected.[1]

This is the kind of intimacy, both internal and external, that this book seeks to help both athletes and the people who train them understand.

Lastly, I would implore you, as you dive into what this book has to offer, to reconsider how you think about clichés, and the sheer quantity thereof, that seem to always crop up when talking about sports and sports training. These are images that have been ingrained in us through cultural osmosis. Sayings about practice making perfect or drive and commitment being key, images of athletes and their teams as sailing crews working together on the high seas or the dire fight of competition being like the dire

---

[1]'Andre Agassi: International Tennis Hall of Fame Induction Address', American Rhetoric, 10 September 2001, https://tinyurl.com/3ehjk5ds. Accessed on 20 February 2023.

fight of war, sheer grit turning the tables for an underdog or matchups like something straight out of a Hollywood screenplay, etc. While none of these sorts of bromides seem particularly useful when trying to figure out, on a technical and emotional level, how to go about training an elite athlete, it bears reminding that all clichés and the analogies that stem from them are based on an undeniable truth. It is not just that practice, teamwork and determination are all vital to the success of an elite athlete's career but that these clichés, much like the position any athlete hopes to reach, are transcendent. They turn out to be true not just in the obvious and general ways anyone would understand them but as the foundational building blocks of a world totally unlike what most people ever get to experience. When you get right down to it, a lot of the philosophy behind genuinely transformative coaching is about invoking clichés in a way that is profound and being able to separate the chaff of banality and overuse from the wheat of the idea's power. Clichés take on an entirely different weight and meaning when the stakes, aim and talent are incredibly high. I will teach you how to use these principles to elevate your players to their greatest heights. Let's begin.

SECTION I

HOW TO GET STARTED AS AN ATHLETE

1

TALENT

There is an urban legend about Pablo Picasso, something more akin to a modern fable than an account of a historical event. The story goes that Picasso was sitting on a bench in a park, enjoying a leisurely afternoon in the warm Parisian breeze. We don't know how old Picasso was at this point, nor what era of his artistic career he was in when this happened. Maybe his acclaimed anti-war piece *Guernica* was already touring internationally or maybe he was beginning to experiment with perspective in a way that would lead to the development of Cubism. Regardless, he was famous enough to be recognized at this point. A young woman approached him on the bench, explaining how deeply she admired his work. She asked, humbly and earnestly, if he would be able to draw a portrait of her. He agreed, took a scrap of paper and, in one masterful line, drew the woman before him. He handed it to her and her face lit up in delight.

'Thank you! This is wonderful. The way you've managed to capture my likeness, my essence, in a single stroke. Simply incredible! How much do I owe you?'

'$5,000.' Picasso was calm, matter of fact.

'What?' The young woman was confused. 'Are you

serious? How could you charge that much for such a tiny portrait? It only took you a minute to draw!'

Picasso is said to have smiled and offered the following retort: 'No, my dear, it took my entire life.'

Regardless of whether or not this actually happened, the story has become a powerful example of the way skill actually works. It helps us understand that the single most harmful misunderstanding about talent is the idea that it emerges from inside someone fully formed, nearly magical in how innate and instinctive it is. This simply isn't true, and the prevalence of this idea tells us a lot about the relationship that spectators have with the talented people that they admire. We have an incredibly deep and incredibly strong urge to view them only as their most surface-level selves, an urge that is stoked by marketing and brand management, since this sense of gobsmacked amazement is so profitable.

But talent doesn't work that way. You are not born better than anyone else at anything, not really. In 1998, a research paper was published in the scientific journal *Behavioral and Brain Sciences* on the validity of the so-called 'talent account', the idea that a person's level of skill at any given task is governed more by a certain amount of relevant intrinsic ability than by external factors such as early experiences, opportunities and training. When they looked at the most relevant and current information from the fields of biology, psychology and sociology, researchers Michael Howe, Jane Davidson and John Sloboda found that while there are some physiological components to a person's level of skill, the idea of the talent account is 'simply over exaggerated and oversimplified', and that a more accurate and responsible version of the idea of talent 'would be a place-holder for the as yet unmapped influence of biology on special expertise'.[1]

Over two decades later, a genetic component directly related to innate talent is yet to be found. Of course, we understand the indirect impact of genetic components, i.e. physical attributes that certain players are born with that give them an edge in their particular sport. Shaquille O'Neal being over 7 ft tall and weighing 324 pounds gave him a clear advantage over other smaller basketball players; whereas Simone Biles being only 4 ft 8 in. tall and weighing only 105 pounds helped her become the most decorated American gymnast of all time.

Beyond these kinds of general static advantages, there can often be the spark of something innate in children: a knack for a certain kind of physical or mental activity that makes itself apparent early on in life. But this kind of ability doesn't mean anything unless it is recognized and honed. The idea of talent existing in a person fully formed is so harmful to young athletes and their parents because it makes them stumble at the first hurdle. This concept fundamentally misunderstands the nature of talent, namely that it takes a lot of work and dedication to encourage it and make it evident. Malcolm Gladwell is famous for his 10,000 hour rule from his book *Outliers* (the idea that you need to clock in at least 10,000 hours of repetition to be an expert at whatever it is you are doing), but this is also a thing people misunderstand. The rule was never meant to imply that 10,000 hours of work automatically makes you

---

[1] Howe, Michael J.A., Jane W. Davidson, and John A. Sloboda, 'Innate Talents: Reality or Myth?', *Behavioral and Brain Sciences*, Vol. 21, No. 3, 1998, pp. 399–442, https://bit.ly/3XkHKC9. Accessed on 9 February 2023.

one of the best at whatever you are working at or that it will make you particularly great, but that, as Gladwell himself later clarified in an online interview, 'natural ability requires a huge investment of time in order to be made manifest'.[2]

The development of talent within someone is more in line with production comparisons than with divine ones. Innate talent is to elite athleticism as oil is to plastic, or a tree is to an ornate desk, or a pile of steel ingots is to a bridge. Talent is a raw material that needs to be shaped and refined, changing forms over time through honing and application along a series of intricate steps in order to turn into exceptional gameplay.

In October 2019, I had the privilege to speak with Dr Kumar Mehta, a brilliant researcher and chief executive officer (CEO). Dr Mehta is an expert in the field of innovation science. His book, the Amazon bestseller, *The Innovation Biome*, is all about how businesses can use the principles of innovation to break out of the constraints of conventional wisdom and create better products while doing social good.

We met because he was trying to break the 'talent code', so to speak, to understand the intricate nature of the way in which talent manifests itself in people across multiple disciplines. We were seated on either side of my desk and he kept getting distracted by the large portraits behind me, pictures of the various star players whom I have trained over the years—Maria Sharapova, Andre Agassi,

[2]Baer, Drake, 'Malcolm Gladwell Explains What Everyone Gets Wrong About His Famous '10,000 Hour Rule', *Business Insider India*, 2 June 2014, https://tinyurl.com/2ft8bbxz. Accessed on 9 February 2023.

Anna Kournikova, Marcelos Rios, Jim Courier, etc. We began talking about the moments when I first became aware of the talents that these athletes possessed—watching Mary Pierce picking up a racket for the first time at age 10 and playing sets on the top courts by the end of that same day; seeing Kei Nishikori play in Japan at age 11, unintimidated by the pros, sponsors and the enormous crowd that came to see him, able to keep up his footwork and groundstrokes with a kind of fearless audacity that made him go for every shot, etc.

I saw an expression of understanding spread across Dr Mehta's face. When his son had been two years old, he had taken him to the doctor for a routine checkup, and while they were in the waiting room, he saw another child his son's age climbing and hopping over chairs and coffee tables with a kind of balance and coordination that Dr Mehta's son wasn't even close to exhibiting. Later on, Dr Mehta would spend a lot of time and money trying to hone his son's sporting abilities, and while his son never hated the games or his involvement in them, they never really clicked and he ended up quitting. His son would later go to a top university in the United States (US) and become a successful engineer. In talking about the identification of nascent talent in children, Dr Mehta was able to realize how much more his son would have benefitted from further encouragement of his apparent mathematical capabilities rather than through his attempts to bolster talent that was not there.

Another example: My son, Christopher, was quickly nicknamed 'Toughy' by the rest of the family, since, after being born prematurely, he showed a tremendous fighting spirit that would become a staple of his personality. When he was 8, he was already bigger and stronger than most of the other kids around him, weighing 130 pounds and putting his size to good use on the field, playing football as a defensive tackle. Toughy's dedication to football was consistent and rigorous. He constantly went through brutal training sessions to improve his play. From a physical standpoint, Toughy had a lot of potential and was even able to reach some of that potential through sheer audaciousness, but what kept him from becoming a great football player was the lack of cognitive skills that are essential for the strategic elements of the sport. He was never able to keep track of the ball and would frequently end up in the wrong position during plays. This is, of course, not to call him too dumb for the sport, but simply to say that his talents lay elsewhere. Through his dedication to the sport, he was able to find out what it was about the game that never managed to click with him, namely the reliance on a team and the subsequent flood of variables that affect every play. He was able to take the skills he developed from his days playing football and apply them to a sport much more suited to his natural temperaments—martial arts. He is a master in Hwa Rang Do, Taekwondo and Ming Wu. We see these things in action—identifying what it is that your child has a knack for and playing to their strengths: a combination of innate talent and hard work.

This leads to another fundamental aspect of developing talent in young children that is often overlooked and misunderstood. While undeniably interwoven, talent and potential are decidedly not the same and they differ significantly between individuals. While these terms are used interchangeably on a colloquial level, there is a big difference between them within the world of sports and sports coaching. Someone's potential for something is the upper limit of their ability to do that thing, whereas someone's talent is the amount of success they find doing that activity based on their ability. This might sound pedantic or maybe even a bit counterintuitive, but this distinction is vital. So much of the mental side of sports training is about properly manipulating perspective for the student, both with regards to themselves and the forces around them, and this is where the understanding that any trace of raw talent, even when honed, doesn't guarantee anything on a one-to-one scale, begins. Someone who isn't very talented at, say, singing, might reach their 'full potential' fairly easily since there are not very many places to go, while someone whose singing ability is much better will have a harder time becoming as good as they know they could be because the possibilities are so much greater. You can think of this dynamic in terms of packing a suitcase for a long trip—potential is the amount of space you have in the suitcase and talent is the amount of clothes, toiletries and other such things that you fill the suitcase with. You can think of the process of training and talent honing as finding the best way to fill the suitcase, whether that be with special folds, hidden pockets or getting more appropriately-sized luggage.

◆

In order to begin shaping a child's athletic talent, there are three general guidelines you should be following as a baseline. Everything in sports training is dependent on the mastery of all the previous steps before it, and these steps, when applied early on in a child's life, provide the most crucial and basic foundations for the rest of their career as well as your role in it.

The first step is to **Identify Your Child's Skills**. This goes beyond the more obvious 'what abilities and functions does my child seem to be exhibiting a knack for?' kind of questions we have already talked about. That kind of integration is, of course, extremely necessary, but you're looking for more than just innate talent. You should also be looking at what it is that your child is actually interested in, what kind of activities they gravitate towards and what kind of situations they do or do not like to be involved in. Recognizing enthusiasm not only saves you a lot of time and money early on, as in in the case of Dr Mehta, but it also sets up a healthy relationship dynamic between you and your child. Because so much of what it takes to train as an elite athlete has to be self-created and should come organically to the child in question; anger, resentment and coercion are totally fatal to a young athlete's career. It is impossible to build a truly great athlete if they don't have a genuine love for the game they are playing. That can come over time, and a good parent knows not to give in to their child's every complaint; this love must come naturally. Of course, there are examples of elite athletes who were made to train for a specific sport starting so early that the parents met no resistance because the child wasn't cognitively developed enough to understand the weight of what they're taking on, like Tracy Austin, whose mother made her start 'playing' tennis at the age of three, and who would go on to not only become No. 1 in the Women's Tennis Association (WTA) in 1980, but also become the youngest US Open female singles champion in history at the age of 17. But, besides the ethical questions behind this method, its efficacy seems to be fairly spotty as well. Make no mistake, beginning a child's training early does give them a significant advantage, but the question is how early should we start training them and what that training looks like. No matter how early you start a child's training, anyone who doesn't already have that aforementioned innate spark to foster will not be able to do what Tracy Austin did. In fact, in many cases, this abusive early start can actually snuff out any spark rather than fan it.

When it comes to what to look for in your child, it's crucial to understand the foundational physical abilities that every child exhibits to a greater or lesser extent—strength, power, balance, coordination and more.

Keep in mind that general physical traits apply to all people in general, but if you understand these traits and your child well enough, you should be able to start reading between the lines of their everyday play and interests and see where they might excel.

These general traits feed into more complicated and sports-specific physical actions in fairly obvious ways. As I mentioned before, all sports training relies on mastering a foundation of skills and this is true even before you bring drills or game rules into a child's life. Some of those actions are as follows—throwing, catching and striking. Sports, such as tennis, require nearly all of these skills, while some other sports, like golf or darts, require only one or two. So, again, knowing the intricacies of the fundamental building blocks of various sports and your child's unique tendencies gives you an edge in every aspect of early training and play.

Like physical skills, there is also a set of developing cognitive or mental skills that a child can display early on—attention span and speed of processing information. And there are a set of more complicated yet fairly self-explanatory cognitive actions vital in different capacities and degrees to every sport. For example, does the child understand the game, see the opportunities of the plays and know where to position themselves? These directly tie back to the building blocks of mental ability mentioned above that you can track as a parent, such as determination and work ethic.

The next step to shaping your child's athletic potential at the very earliest stages is to **become familiar with your local sports culture.** This requires a lot of research from you as the parent. It is important to not only be asking questions about what resources your local sports scene has to help with the growth of a child athlete but also to find the hard answers—What sports are supported and highly regarded in my area? Where can I find professionals to help train my child in the sport they seem to be excelling in? How good are these trainers? How much do they cost? Will I have to move to get my child the training they deserve? Is there a university in the area that could provide scholarships if my child doesn't end up going pro? Will my child still have options, athletic or otherwise, if we stay put? These questions are tough and the answers are not always straightforward, but they are absolutely vital to your child's success. Later on, in Section V of this book, you will find an entire chapter dedicated to talking about a parent's role in their child's journey to becoming an elite athlete, but for now, I will just say that a parent has the most direct control over their child's health and success in these early years; and these kinds of hard questions, asked with an eye toward both your child's success and your child's happiness and well-being, are going to be the foundation of your entire relationship with your child's professional life, so seek the truth with honesty and humility.

This kind of research also gives two additional advantages in the early stages of your child's journey. Firstly, you'll be able to learn a lot about the nuances and ins and outs of the industry by staying informed, even about things that might seem inconsequential but that actually, under the right circumstances, are very helpful. For example, if a child born in December of one year and a child born in January in the following year are both trying to train and compete in the junior rankings, the one born in January will, generally speaking, have the edge. Despite the fact that the child born in December is only a month older than the second child, they will often be competing with children a year younger than them in tournaments, and because of the rapidly changing physiological state of young kids, a year can often mean wildly different physical and cognitive abilities. It has the potential to make or break a game or a match, which can affect the child's win–loss ratio—one of the few things that scouters and coaches and potential sponsors look at besides the quality of the individual components of their gameplay, as it is one of the few stats they have to go off of at such an early stage. None of this is guaranteed, of course, but it is things like this that would fly over the heads of less involved parents and which more informed ones can plan and strategize around.

The second reason this kind of research is beneficial is much less convoluted. It is essentially a statistical fact that getting your child professional athletic training early on gives them a significant edge in the competition. Doing research allows you to make informed decisions about coaches and programmes. The next chapter is all about early specialization, so I won't go into too much detail here, but know that getting a child who shows promise and genuine interest in a sport professional training by the age of five or six is crucial in the making of an elite athlete.

The third step to honing your child's talent and positively shaping the earliest stages of their athletic journey is to **understand and follow trainability windows.** These are exactly what they sound like—the type of training and focus that should be given to the child during each window of time in their development. The so-called physiological window or window of opportunity is defined as such because it represents the ideal moment to favour the rapid optimization of learning and increase in performance. The first phase goes from two–four years of age, and from there, the child keeps growing according to the specific sports.

Of course, there is a larger truth hanging over this final frontier of athletic development, which is that this top position, much like talent itself, is not static. It's ever changing and ever shifting as the player's career waxes and wanes as they constantly and consistently improve. This isn't just because rankings are established on a rolling basis, only counting points earned from the last 52 weeks, but because the road to becoming a truly great elite athlete is not linear. It is paved with seemingly endless amount of games, meets, matches and tournaments, each one built on the accumulated foundations of all their past experience. An athlete at this level must be constantly growing internally and externally, fostering their talent in everything they do, striving to do better and push themselves, even in the face of losses. They must meet and conquer every obstacle presented to them with their knowledge and expertise because the process of continuous improvement is never-ending.

2

EARLY SPECIALIZATION

There is almost always some kind of innate proclivity to certain kinds of actions in young athletes that could be called 'talent', but the way talent actually manifests itself and becomes relevant is much more about external factors well within the control of the athlete, their parents, the coaches, etc. One of these factors is timing. The rigours of elite athleticism are extremely intense as to make true greatness virtually inaccessible to all but a small handful of people, partly because the core mental and physical elements of an athlete's composure require honing from the very earliest stages of their development. The mind and body are most malleable in the first decade of a person's life and so it is crucial that parents and the coaches they hire strike while the iron's hot.

If we go back to our production analogies from the previous chapter, timing plays a key role in the series of intricate steps that transforms ingots into beams into bridges. We can think about the production of fruit and fruit products as well. Think of how many steps it takes to, say, create a bottle of wine. Planting, growing and harvesting the grapes, extracting their juice, fermentation and filtration, and aging, not to mention bottling the wine and having to actually sell it once it's been created. Timing obviously plays a huge role in every step of the process since organic matter like fruit is perishable, but there are a whole host of time-sensitive decisions that have to be made even before we pick the first grape off the vine. We have to figure out the proper season to plant, what kind of wine we want to make, what kind of grapes we want to use and what our vineyard is going to look like. How are we going to create enough space for the grapes to mature properly? What financial deals with manufacturers/distributors do we need to strike in order to fund and sell the product we eventually hope to make? How are we going to balance the cost of production against future revenue so that we turn a profit?

All of these steps have to be completed before we truly begin the wine-making process, and this kind of extensive preparation is the same principle behind early specialization in sports. The idea is simple—a child can excel much more at a sport if they focus on said sport exclusively from the earliest stages of their development.

The mother of my children is American and she believed in an 'all-rounder' style of sports involvement that is very popular in the US. The idea is to get the child to play as many sports as possible, changing games with various seasons, in order to have them try a whole host of options to see what they like. My children played football, soccer, gymnastics, tennis and golf while also taking art classes and other similar extracurricular activities. Despite having athletic qualities, by the time they all turned 12, they turned out to be mediocre at sports, jacks of all trades; and since they didn't feel particularly drawn to any sport, all three of them gave up entirely.

This type of schedule can work on a casual level, mainly for parents who aren't really worried about their child's relative skill at any given sport but are more focussed on the social, physical and psychological benefits that participating in sports in general can give their children. But if you want your child to become a true athlete, early specialization is mandatory.

Research supports this. In 2005, a study was done by Mia McCorkel and Audrey Bockerstette, 2 students at the University of Arizona, in order to find out what the potential benefits of early specialization in sports would be. They predicted that early specialization would contribute to an athlete's success and they were correct. Only 12 per cent of those surveyed who did not specialize early were successful, meaning they found favour among recruiters and were granted scholarships, while nearly 60 per cent of those surveyed who had specialized early were successful. They reported that: 'This result was correctly predicted despite many expert and doctor opinions, which claimed that playing multiple sports is more beneficial. The benefits of early specialization might be due to developing talent in the chosen sport. However, success from early specialization may also be due to the many opportunities it provides to have talent noticed by college recruiters more than an athlete who plays only part time.'[3] For our purposes, this distinction isn't really important. Whether early specialization helps

---

[3]McCorkel, Mia and Audrey Bockerstette, *A Study to Determine the Impact of Early Specialization on Athletic Success*, 16 May 2005, University of Arizona, Research Project, https://bit.ly/40CgNNj. Accessed on 9 February 2023.

with developing ability or helps with showcasing that ability to various sponsors, both play off of one another and are invaluable to the process.

Now, this study certainly isn't the be-all and end-all. It is the result of a survey given out to a decent-sized, but by no means definitive, pool of people. The study acknowledges its limitations, but even with everything left to be explored, the idea is solid and intuitive—getting a head start with serious and specific training is bound to be advantageous in any field. If the disparity in these numbers can be so large on the university level, then we can imagine that the difference is all the more pronounced among the much higher skill plateau of professionals.

This is not to say that a child should only ever play one sport, quite the opposite. Cross-training, the practice of seriously training in one sport while still allowing the athlete to play other sports casually, is vital for proper growth. By playing different sports and adopting different strategies for them, the young athlete is able to stay mentally and physically sharp while avoiding burnout. When applied properly, cross-training turns these other sports into something closer to elaborate exercises or fun ways to cut loose while staying active. The key to early specialization is that a young athlete as well as their support systems and all the broader financial/ temporal resources they provide, should be seriously dedicated to one sport exclusively and not be necessarily trapped or limited to only ever playing that sport. Like anything else, however, cross-training is best applied in moderation.

Of course, there are a handful of errant examples of pro players who seemed to be equally talented in two sports for a large part of their early careers before deciding on one to pursue. Famously, Roger Federer had to make a choice between tennis and soccer as did LeBron James between basketball and football. But obviously, since these examples are 2 of the greatest athletes not only in the history of their sports but in all sports, this is extremely rare to the point of being negligible, which makes serious training in multiple sports not an advisable strategy at all.

The other reason early specialization is important when training to become an elite athlete is that individual sports like swimming, golf and tennis are much more specialized than team sports. There's no particular position you have to fill and no one else you can rely on. Everything falls on you and you alone. Learning to play the game well means adapting your play style to all sorts of nuances and counter moves. Because the athletes are by themselves, these sports become more total and holistic for them, and tennis is perhaps the most demanding in terms of interactivity, strategy and physicality. These individual and highly technical sports present a challenge when transitioning from one sport to another, no matter how good the individual is as an athlete. Therefore, early specialization is a critical factor in harnessing and maximizing the skills of the young aspiring high performer.

We can also think about early specialization like we think about learning a language. The child's mind is biologically better prepared to learn the complexities of a new language as it is still in the earliest stages of developing those parts of the brain. This is why you often see children raised in households with two spoken languages become effectively bilingual by the time they begin to speak with any kind of regularity. Contrast this with trying to learn a new language as an adult. Even with a more structured and streamlined approach, with plotted out learning curves regarding vocabulary and grammar rules, it is exponentially harder because the most absorbent parts of our brains have cooled off, became fully developed and thus locked into our norms, making them less malleable. All this information will be new and viewed through the lens of our 'natural' language, rather than being worked in as a part of that language early on. The same principle applies to all the physical, and to a lesser extent, cognitive demands of elite athleticism.

Hearing all of this, you might be wondering more about the moral implications: Is it right to start a child on such a difficult and intense life path before they or their brains are fully developed and before they have the awareness to offer their consent? This is a very understandable concern. You hear things like the Tracy Austin story from the previous chapter, or the prevalent and unfortunately racially-coded trope of the so-called 'tiger mom' traumatizing their children, or you read Agassi's memoir and see how much he says he hated tennis and how hard and early his father pushed him. You hear about how Agassi's father had him batting balloons in his highchair to train his hand–eye coordination at two years old, and you can't help but question whether or not this kind of early training is inherently abusive.

While it is true that there are, undoubtedly, a lot of parents who try and masquerade their abuse and obsession as simply rigorous investment in their child's success, this is not the norm; and this kind of manipulation only ever hurts an athlete in both the long and short term. Early specialization is not an inherently abusive strategy since in order to implement it properly, you must keep up healthy and cooperative communication with your child. This section has a chapter that exclusively focusses on communication as a fundamental part of the coaching process, but for our purposes here, it's important to note that your job is to encourage and tease out what you already see in your child. There is a big difference between forcing a two- or three-year-old child down the path that you have decided is going to be their future and cutting off any avenue that may lead to a life outside of the sport, and in exposing your child to a variety of activities at an early age, seeing which they like most and are best at and then getting the professional help they need in order to support that passion. The reality is that all the external pressure and guidance in the world won't help athletes who are not invested in becoming great themselves. Again, many of the core elements of an athlete's play must be crafted and spurred on by engines that are internal and self-made.

These things can be hard to parse out though, especially when looking at a parent–child relationship from the outside. In the case of Agassi, I know that he didn't seem to hate tennis when I was training him, and that it would, in my professional opinion, be impossible to reach the heights Agassi did while maintaining a complete and total hate of the sport. How a child feels about these things can often also shift over time, changing as they go through life. I say this all, however, fully acknowledging the almost monomaniacal intensity of his father's training and the lasting psychological effects that it has had.

What's most important is maintaining a compassionate dynamic with your child. A perceptive parent can see, even at their child's youngest age, the early blossoms of clear preference and engagement, and they can also see these things grow and shift as more opportunities are given to the child. This kind of training is not about you; it's about your child and how to embrace and bolster their talents in the best and most healthy ways.

My brother Jorge and I come from a very athletic family. My mother was an Olympic swimming coach, and Jorge and I swam and played tennis and golf during our childhoods. When I was eight and my brother was seven, our parents took us out to a formal dinner and explained the situation to us. They gave us all the pros and cons of pursuing sports on a high-performance level and asked us if we were interested in this kind of commitment. My brother and I were so fired up, we were more than happy to agree. Our parents made us choose a sport to focus on. Jorge chose swimming and I chose tennis. Jorge would go on to compete in the 1972 and 1976 Olympics, and I, of course, would go on to have the career that I do. Needless to say, the conversations you have with your children don't have to be as ceremonial as what my family did, but the contents of the conversations should be similar. You should make your child aware of both the good and the bad so you can work toward reaching a consensus together.

The last thing I want to touch on with regards to early specialization is the idea of burnout. I mentioned it earlier when talking about cross-training, and it's an idea worth diving into because, like so much else in the world of elite athletic training, it is often misunderstood. Conventional wisdom says that burnout happens when training is done too early and too hard; the athlete becomes overworked, begins to hate the game and eventually quits.

This isn't how burnout actually works. Of course, coaches, parents and trainers need to be aware of a child's physical limits and make sure to train them in ways that push up against said limits without injuring or otherwise harming the athlete, but that's true at every stage of a player's career. It is worth noting that drop out and burnout are not the same thing. Many players drop out of the sport by reaching a plateau through selection funneling, and this is, for some athletes of a certain skill level, fairly natural. Likewise, being overworked and being burnt out are not the same thing. In my experience, burnout is almost exclusively a result of mental and emotional stresses piling up, causing a loss of motivation. This ties back into my point about internal engines and a parent's role in supporting their function. The 2 things that most contribute to burnout are unreasonably high external expectations and unyielding parental pressure, direct and indirect, which are both caused in large part by a lack of compassion for and communication with the athlete in question from the various members of their support group. This is entirely avoidable and has nothing to do with early specialization.

Your job as a parent has many layers and facets, some of which might not be readily apparent to your children until much later in their lives. One of the most central roles of a parent, as a team leader, is that of the protector, the one who looks out for a player and their well-being, working with them and their team to build a healthy and cooperative foundation for their success. By implementing early specialization in a proper and mindful way, you can improve all of your athlete's abilities and help fuel their motivation, on and off the playing field.

3

SEQUENCE AND SPHERES

As I previously mentioned, one of the core elements of elite sports training, and indeed sports training of virtually any kind, is the process of mastering all the preceding components of a goal in order to use that intimate experience to reach said goal. The beauty of this kind of development is that the theory applies to every aspect of the game, regardless of scale or scope. On the micro level, you might focus on each part of a certain movement, stroke or swing (position, angle, follow through, speed, accuracy, etc.) to be able to employ an increasingly refined version of said swing and then go on to focus on making that swing near-automatic in order to use it in more situations. On a macro level, we can think of competition or official rankings: the idea of a selection funnel—only those who prove themselves to be the cream of the crop can move on to the next stage, on and on, into an ever-smaller pool of players—quarterfinals, playoffs, championships, top 100, top 10 to the best in the world.

I have used terms like 'building' and 'constructing' when referring to the development of children into elite athletes. I do this not as a way to be overly clinical or to dehumanize the players, but as a way to reflect this core truth of the process. Construction is another key analogy to keep in mind. If you consider some of the grandest architectural achievements in the world, buildings like the Taj Mahal, the Burj Khalifa or the Eiffel Tower; they all had not only extensive planning and long construction cycles carried out and overseen by hundreds, if not thousands of people, but they are all able to remain structurally sound because the process was methodical, logical and patient. The minds behind these great structures, as well as the workers who physically built them, made a clear plan and saw it through without getting ahead of themselves. They understood that their grand vision couldn't become a reality unless they worked from the ground up, completing the foundations before moving on to the next step. So it is with elite athletes. There is, simply put, no way to hack a blueprint, no way to cheat the system in order to achieve your goals. The only way out of your current rank, plateau and skill range is to follow the arduous path through it without compromise.

Because this idea of sequencing is so vital to the athletic process, I have compiled a blueprint of success—10 steps that can be applied both to large career goals as well as smaller mechanical tweaks. Let's analyse those steps one by one.

It should be obvious that a solid vision of what you want to achieve is mandatory to any mission, and this first foundational element is where **imagination** comes in. Later on, in Section IV, there is an entire chapter dedicated to the role of dreams in an elite athlete's life, but the main point right now is that there is almost no better motivator for a young player than their dream of success. Your job as a parent or a coach is to stoke that dream, turn it from a spark to an ember to a roaring fire and to do so in a way that is healthy, communicative and realistic for the child.

There is a major and yet sometimes very slight difference between dreams as means to spur on improved gameplay and dreams as a means to maintain delusion. This means that it is up to the mentors to help guide an athlete's self-image, allowing their imagination to soar in every facet of their training, while also reining in those feelings of grandeur when appropriate to keep them realistically inspired. This is especially true in the early stages when a child doesn't have very many concrete achievements to reassure them of their skill. I cannot count how many times I've heard a young player say things like: 'With this shot, I'll beat Serena!' or 'This is Ronaldo's free kick!' or 'Here comes Curry's 3 pointer!'

Do this properly and you'll be able to see a child's ambition grow naturally, going from dreaming of winning difficult games to winning whole tournaments. To make use of another analogy, we can think about imagination as the roots of the young athlete's career. This is what, in the most trying and turbulent moments of their career, will keep them anchored and chasing their dream.

The concept of **duplication** is a fairly straightforward one: Every action that an athlete does during the course of an actual game is the latest in an increasingly long line of copies of an original move. Your serve, your backhand, your return—everything is a copy of a copy of a copy, hundreds of thousands of copies deep, ad nearly infinitum. It is absolutely paramount that these moves be practised over and over and over again, so many times that a player's prowess goes beyond simple mastery and becomes automatic, like a machine that is able to produce identical versions of the same thing every single time. In order for this to happen, the copies that a player is working with have to be clean, clear and perfect, and the only way for that to happen is a lot of time and a lot of constant repetition.

Continuity may seem to be very similar to duplication at first, but it's important to know that they are not the same thing. While duplication deals with the repetition of specific mechanical motions, continuity refers to keeping up consistency within the more general realm of practice itself. It is the idea that a player needs to keep a schedule and that the only way to reach the great heights they aspire to is to constantly be growing by practising regularly. This might seem like a no-brainer, and it almost certainly is, but it's also a core part of an elite athlete's lifestyle that needs to be instilled early on. This, like many things in the process of training elite athletes, applies on both a macro and micro scale. Everything, from training hours and what days you take off to what drills and activities you do and what you eat needs to be scheduled, monitored and kept up. This is not to say that an athlete's training schedule will never change, because increasing skill demands it to, but the principle is the same—continuity in everything you do.

Order is what I was talking about earlier; the methodical sequence in which various things need to be built and established before a player and their support system can move on to the next component. **Adjustments**, then, we can imagine as detours from that general plan or smaller plans that crop up due to the natural evolution of an athlete's career, different parts of their gameplay need to be...well, adjusted.

The thing about these types of small improvements is that, since the climb to excellence is never-ending even once you've reached it and there are always ways to improve your playing, a player that is actually progressing and growing will always have to keep making these adjustments. If they aren't, then something is wrong. Small change is constant and vital.

Prioritizing is another facet of properly structured training. What elements are we going to improve first? What is most vital? Do we focus on strengths to cover weaknesses or work on the weaknesses first so they don't need to be covered at all? What is best for the player's gameplay and overall career? These kinds of questions can only be answered with the kind of honest and thorough analysis that comes with the intimate knowledge of a player and their history in the sport. Correct prioritization greatly increases an athlete's rate of growth, since all the proverbial pieces fall into place in a sequence that makes the most sense and has the most impact. You can think of order and prioritizing as two sides of the same coin. Order is proactive and preemptive, whereas prioritizing is reactive, always shifting with the needs of the player.

Though imagination sustains an athlete on a macro scale, only **achievements** can keep an athlete on top of the daily grind to excellence. These accomplishments can be large or small, anything from doing well in a tournament to learning and applying something new, but they are tangible reminders of the athlete's skill and are a key force in driving the athlete to keep working to succeed. Notice how I am not simply talking about victories. In an athlete's life, especially early in their career, it is inevitable that they

will suffer defeats for a variety of reasons, both in and out
of their control. Not only are these losses vital in carving a
player's character and composure, but they also provide an
invaluable learning experience that can be another type of
achievement if the athlete is willing to humble themselves
enough to receive the lesson. A balance of wins and losses
is healthy. Players who lose too much get discouraged and
quit, whereas players who win too much get complacent
and overestimate their ability.

Assessment is exactly what it sounds like—an
examination of the latest match, tournament, training
session, etc., through a lens of honesty and assisted
growth. These matches should be broken down within the
context of the player's entire career, the highs and the lows
they've experienced in the past. As I mentioned earlier,
this requires deep knowledge and a deep relationship
with not only the player, but with every member of their
support system and every aspect of their gameplay. The
athlete must also, of course, know themselves. Again, like
every other factor of this sequence, this principle should be
applied on large and small scale, even on a point-to-point
basis during a game, constantly analysing the situation and
adapting accordingly.

The role of **conclusion** and **excellence** in this blueprint
is virtually the same as the 'train to win' and 'train for
excellence' sections of the teachability windows in Chapter
1. Conclusion is all about realizing a player's dream through
the application of all the previous steps, while Excellence
is the constant striving to become even greater than that.
Excellence is, again, like perfection, a constantly moving
target that an athlete reaches in waves as they and the

world around them fluctuates with the forces of an incomprehensible number of variables.

These factors, and the idea of what is and is not in the athlete's control, bring us to another key idea of sports training—the three spheres. There are three parts to an athlete's game that determine the potency of their gameplay over all—the physical sphere, the mental sphere and the competitive sphere. Due to the nature of the things demanded by each one, these three spheres must be accessed in a certain order. Once an athlete starts seriously competing, the work shifts. It stops being about simply accessing these components and more about bolstering each of them in a way that does not become too lopsided. All these areas must be worked on together, as separate parts of one whole unit, in order for any individual element to really work. The physical influences the mental as they both influence the competitive, and then, once an athlete gets the results, the competitive feeds directly back into the mental and physical. These spheres and the relationships they have with one another are vital and very nearly infinite. Like with talent, achievements and excellence, these areas never stop growing and developing just like the player. The sequences of development outlined in this chapter are linear in how they progress, but the ways in which they are applied are so numerous and so varied that the processes are, really, theories in flux and ideas with infinite application.

SECTION II

FUNDAMENTALS

4

PLANNING

When I first saw Jim Courier practice, I instantly knew there was something special not just about him, but also his work ethic. He was a tall and muscular kid, just 15 years old, who put everything he had into every sprint and drill, and he was constantly leaving everybody behind on all counts. Beyond that, you could see in his face as he moved swiftly around the court that he had no hang-ups or preoccupations about what others might think of him. He was unbothered, never expecting praise or outside encouragement; he judged himself and adhered only to that judgment. You could feel his desire to improve.

Later, after practice, I called him into my office in order to learn more about him. I asked him what his goal was. He looked me in the eye, his gaze intense and unflinching, and simply said that he was going to be the best in the world. I asked him how he was going to do that, to which he confidently responded: 'With your help. How are you going to do that?'

The question became stuck in my head and I spent the rest of the evening and the entirety of that night devising a plan to ensure Jim's success. We met in my office the next day and I explained what was going to happen. I told him that I could help him become the best in the world, but that he would have to follow the programme I proposed to him in order for it to work. It was a training regimen that had seen much success in the world of Olympic sports but had never been adapted for tennis. After I gave him a rough outline of my idea, he agreed enthusiastically. I assigned Sergio Cruz to be his coach, and over the next few days, the three of us worked together to flesh out my design and develop a concrete five-year plan.

We followed the plan diligently. Jim avoided injury by never overdoing anything. He worked tirelessly, giving his all to everything, staying motivated and constantly improving. After a few years, he caught up to and beat Agassi and Pete Sampras. He achieved his first major goal—to compete in the finals of the French Open. He became our first student to win a grand slam event and, eventually, the first to become world No. 1. Jim had always been full of grit and motivation, but he attributes a lot of his success to our periodization plan early in his career.

◆

Training Blocks, also known as periodization planning, is a strict and detailed training programme based around methodical and incremental improvement over a long period of time by focussing on an athlete's specific skill set and connecting smaller short-term goals up with important tournaments. The aim is to create a system that goes beyond just general improvement strategies and makes goals tactile and attainable.

Training should, in all reality, function the way a Global Positioning System (GPS) does. You may be able to reach your destination through vague and static directions (take I-270 west past X; turn right once you see Y; it's on the next street over from Z, etc.) or even a large general map of the area, but the roadmap you create in order to get there should be dynamic and specific, tailored to your athlete's specific journey, able to change and adapt as the player's career evolves over time with its invariable ups and downs. When you make a wrong turn, a GPS pivots, adjusts and tells you how to still get to your goal from your new position. It should be the same with this kind of training.

The main philosophical principle behind periodization planning is the need to understand, compare and reflect on the 2 most vital parts of your quest—what you have now and what you still need. The idea is to work backwards, to trace from your goals to your actual abilities and outline the appropriate steps to get there. This is why concrete goals are so important, both on a micro and a macro level. They provide a clear destination for you to plan around. The steps to become the best in the world are much broader and grand than, say, the steps to winning a specific tournament, which are grander and wide-reaching than the steps to master a certain stroke. Regardless of what the size of the goal is, the process of planning and breaking down steps is the same. This brings us to the idea of the Russian nesting dolls, back to building on smaller versions of the same system to establish fundamentals.

What periodization planning also highlights for young athletes is the weight and importance of time. Reaching their most lofty goals takes time and this kind of training regimen reinforces ideas of patience and diligence while allowing them to also see and learn from consistent success as well as from not always gaining victories, since genuine development should take priority over merely winning. Time is a key ingredient to an elite athlete's success, and focussing on time is what periodization planning does better than any other programme.

Any athlete can apply this example of specific planning to any sport. You start from where you want to go, and from there, return, taking into account the development and the results. The important thing is to have a specific written plan with macro and micro goals. This plan is malleable; it is modified as the athlete reaches each of the goals set. It is almost impossible to set a goal as difficult as reaching the top without having a detailed map showing the path and the signs that guide us. If the plan is not in writing, it is not a plan; it is just a mirage. Many coaches have a written plan, but the tricky part is to follow it.

Jorge, the swimmer, planned to compete in the Olympics after four years of planning, with development goals such as improving the double butterfly kick, starts and turns. Simultaneously, result-oriented goals, such as improving the times in 100 m and 200 m butterfly. As a sport, swimming is handled in a more scientific way, where all data is cataloged continuously, analysed and compared—practice times, competition times and even blood counts. A thousandth of a second can be everything in swimming, and hence, planning from start to finish is essential.

The swimming team reviewed and compared the videos taken underwater to study the technical part of the movement, comparing it with the best swimmers. They also had access to the times of other swimmers in training, training camps and high competitions. All these comparisons helped the coaching staff make the necessary adjustments in their training planning. Elite athletes are part of their planning from an early age.

Another vital part of training is understanding the athlete and how he absorbs that training from the psychological point of view. The athlete has to know what phase of training he is in. There are five phases—adaptation, technique, pre-competition, competition and rest. Each phase lasts for approximately three weeks. Some athletes like to know the specific type of training, the volume and intensity loads before daily practices. Others prefer to not get the information so they do not have a predisposition before starting. We need to understand our athletes thoroughly and realize how they respond best to training.

The scheduling of tournaments is one of the most crucial parts of the development of an athlete and periodization planning is done based on the tournament calendar.

First, every tournament should be working towards the goal. One of the most prominent mistakes coaches and parents make is selecting the wrong events. For example, if the goal is to play Nationals in a year, every tournament we play should help us get there; if it does not, it is a waste of time, money and effort.

Secondly, we use the Fibonacci formula, the numerical sequence formed by the sum of the two numbers that precede it, i.e., 1+1=2, 1+2=3, 2+3=5 successively. This is part of nature in patterns of leaf spirals and seeds and it is also found in architecture and art. We can participate in one, two or three trials, but never four in a row. This progression avoids injury and keeps athletes fit and hungry for competition.

Third, not all tournaments have the same importance and that is critical to consider as the levels of preparation are different.

The planning is made well in advance, taking into account all the necessary steps. As the competition approaches, training loads are reduced and the information turns to tactics. The goal is to reach optimal performance at a precise time.

After 10 weeks of training following a competition, it is recommended that the athlete take a break. The final stage is the simplest and the most vital—rest. Rest is essential to developing both the mental and physical spheres, helping to mould a player's mindset and aid in muscular recovery. A player can engage in active rest, where they continue to practise a sport but on a much lower level of intensity and only for fun, or they can take some time off completely. It would be best to build in time for your athlete to rest, allowing optimal recovery.

This planning may seem very complicated, but it is much more intuitive in practice than it looks. The key is to develop a written plan toward the primary goal. Then, divide the programme into yearly segments, using several events during a calendar year, again differentiating the importance levels and not being afraid of changing things when they need to be re-evaluated. The athlete should aim to peak for only four main tournaments and the rest are preparation.

The most important component to implementing this kind of training is communication. As a coach, it isn't helpful in the long run to just draft a plan on your own and force the player to do it. This kind of detailed planning needs to be worked on together. This may seem obvious, but if

I make a plan, it is my plan, whereas if we work together to make a plan, it becomes ours and changes the dynamic in the player's mind. This kind of training should always be collaborative.

As a parent, you should always demand a written schedule for any potential coach you're considering, since anyone worth your time will know the importance of this kind of planning. It is not just some vague idea, but a concrete plan written out to the day. Not only does it prove they are taking you and your child seriously, but it also shows professionalism and knowledge that are an absolute must in the world of sports training. It goes back to what I was saying about Sequencing in Chapter 3—building anything, especially a sturdy and intricate structure, requires planning, forethought and a willingness to change course if something isn't working. It is simply not possible to become a high-ranking athlete or to even really complete any meaningful short-term goals without a plan that is not only detailed, but also flexible, unique and adaptable. The plan or periodization is the foundation on which the construction of an elite athlete is based.

5

VOLUME

Throughout the process of training an elite athlete, it is essential to understand how the training load is managed and assimilated—through Volume, Intensity, Duration and others. When we speak of high volume, we refer to the amount of time dedicated to all aspects of the training that each sport requires as well as to the performance levels.

One example of the high Volume value was Gary Player, a South African golfer, who was always one of the shortest players on whatever tour he was on. However, he believed that he could still compete and do well through the sheer Volume of his practice. Gary didn't miss a workout—even on a rainy day, he managed to hit the range. As a result, he was one of the few players in history to ever win a career Grand Slam.

Indeed, this was something I had seen in my own travels to scout various up-and-coming athletes in different countries—the main difference in skill level simply came down to a matter of Volume. The students who only practised intensely for four to five hours a week never had a chance. Most elite athletes train with continuity for a minimum of 18 hours a week. So every time Gary visited the academy, I asked him to give a talk to motivate the students. For weeks after, everybody at the academy practised as much and as often as they could with unparalleled enthusiasm.

At an early age, the windows of trainability are small and changes occur quickly, hence, the critical importance of not missing training. A child who does not attend the practice or is inconsistent misses out. Their friends improve more quickly. When young athletes, all very competitive, realize that others have developed better skills, they usually choose to leave the sport. Parents have to be very disciplined. First, they have to take them to their daily practices and motivate them never to miss a single scheduled training. One of the essential characteristics of Volume is Continuity. Therefore, it is useless if the student trains 20 hours in one week and only two in the next one, if that student follows different coaching and training systems. It is much more productive to have a continuous progression of the process. Therefore, the priority is training Volume with continuity and a purpose. It is much more effective to work consistently for short periods than to spend many hours training ocassionally.

While talking about the fundamental building blocks of elite athletic training, we need to define several terms that relate to Volume and note how they play into one another. Many parents are very involved in their children's athletic careers, and athletic understanding definitions are essential to communicate better with coaches and child athletes. In addition, most parents devote significant time to their children's sports, becoming team leaders.

Volume is the amount of training that you do, defined as the number of days multiplied by the number of hours.

Similar to the difference between talent and potential that I discussed in Chapter 1, a lot of these terms are used haphazardly on a colloquial level but they have very specific meanings when one is talking about sports training. Understanding this brings us to one of the most crucial aspects of developing effective training schedules—Volume manipulation. You can think of all types of practice having two different interrelated axes—Volume and Intensity. The amount of training and how physically demanding it is called Workload.

Adjusting the Workload based on the situation is key. Working on stroke mechanics might demand many hours of work, at a slow pace or a high Volume with low Intensity. In contrast, preparing for competition, the athlete works fewer hours but gives a 100 per cent or low Volume with high Intensity. Therefore, you have to be able to identify the needs of the athlete and adjust the Workload accordingly.

Not only that, but you also need to be aware of your athlete's personal style and physical inclinations. You need to be able to recognize what works best for them and apply the appropriate amount of Volume. For example, Jorge, the Olympic swimmer, swam around 12,000 m a day when he was training, but Mark Spitz, a swimmer who competed in the same events as Jorge and who won seven gold medals all in world record time, practised only half that distance. The difference was his Intensity. He trained for less time but with greater Intensity.

It is easy to look at Spitz's success and deduce that high Intensity is the best way to practise, but this is a dangerous assumption. When Jorge and his coaches tried to adapt his training to more closely match Spitz's, it didn't work.

Jorge is not the kind of athlete who can train in this way. Nevertheless, Jorge never dropped the level of Quality.

The difference between Intensity and Quality is a matter of which sphere you are referring to. Intensity is a physical component (heart rate, oxygen consumption, etc.), whereas Quality is a mental component (concentration, attention, focus, etc.).

For most athletes, it is not feasible to train at 100 per cent Intensity most of the time. We can think of a racing car driving at full speed on a track. If there is a sudden turn or change to be made, the driver will likely crash if he does not slow down. Driving too slowly can cause an accident. Of course, there is a time and place for maximum speed or for slowing down, but that's the point. You have to know where the athlete is and what he needs and adjust accordingly. Training at 70 per cent is typical for most athletes, especially given the tendency of young athletes to overcorrect. They will often try to increase their Intensity by moving their feet quickly to increase their heart rate. But, at the same time, they move their arms quickly, losing precision and coordination in their haste. It is much more challenging to steer a car when you are going at top speed and the control you manage to exert with your arms is choppy, sudden and clumsy. At the same time, if you go too slowly, you can fall asleep. These setbacks and misunderstandings need to be foreseen and balanced when they inevitably come up. Every athlete is different in assimilating training to achieve their best performance. But, unfortunately, one of the most common mistakes coaches make is that they assume that all athletes embody workload and volumes of information in the same way.

Another advantage of Volume manipulation is that it helps protect the athlete from mental and physical exhaustion and injury. This is another aspect of training that can be difficult to understand when you see the genius of a Roger Federer, Cristiano Ronaldo or Mia Hamm on the move and how they have maintained their quality of play, enthusiasm and have remained relatively injury-free. As a coach, especially in the early stages of an athlete's career, you know better than they do about what training, Volume and Intensity manipulations are necessary for long-term improvement and growth.

Monica Seles is still the single most talented person I've ever trained, and yet her perfectionism toward her mechanics once got the best of her. When she was 14, she wanted to change the mechanics of her forehand stroke—from her two-handed stroke to a more flexible and dynamic one-handed stroke—and kept practising far beyond what we told her to. As a result, she injured herself and was out of commission for months. There is a similar story about Agassi. He wanted to prove he could make the necessary adjustments to his second serve in no time at all—changes to his toss, his grip and the overall motion. He would fail again and again, simply because these are things that take time and many hours of practice to become engrained, but he refused to quit and his attempts got worse as he wore himself out. I pulled him aside and asked him to quit, but he refused. I finally had to put my foot down and demand that he stop for fear of injury. This is why Volume control is so important.

One of the great fortunes as a coach is the proximity to other great coaches from different sports, like Gary Gilchrist, a South African coach who dedicated his life to his golfers. He trained some of the best players in the world. I remember the hours he spent preparing Michelle Wie West and then Paula Kramer and the repetitions with each iron, bunker shot, approach and putting. The goal was to obtain Automatization of the stroke mechanics, only obtained via Volume multiplied by Repetition. After that, it was a matter of Volume manipulation and rehearsing for the world's biggest stages.

It is also worth pointing out that a good sign of an institution that knowing what they are doing is that they not only have a solid periodization plan written down for at least a year in the future, but also include varying volumes of training that increase over time. This points to another component of Volume manipulation—in order for Volume to be effective, it has to have rigorously maintained continuity. You have to be able to gradually yet markedly improve and grow over time and that requires a detailed plan that builds organically on itself.

All these ideas also apply to information as well, not just to physical training. As a player grows and gets older, their knowledge of the game should increase with them and it is up to their coach to funnel this information to them and their gameplay in a way that is manageable while also expanding beyond what has been established. Besides a physical plateau and abusive training tactics, the first thing that stops children from becoming engrained in an athletic community and eventually achieving greatness is being overwhelmed by a flood of information that is too much for their current position in the game. This flood exacerbates their anxieties, fears and wrecks the mental aspects of their game before they have gotten used to how the various spheres of their gameplay intersect. All their potential slowly peters out as they look further and further inward in a recursive and unproductive way. The trainer must protect the student by exercising appropriate control over the volume of information. This balance will take some time to find and achieve consistently and effectively.

The last key factor for Volume manipulation is finding and implementing things that allow you to adjust the Volume in the way you need. This includes a variety of things, for example, enrolling a child in a virtual school. Today, most high-performance athletes worldwide use online schools, which give them the flexibility to split their training into two blocks a day to ensure maximum assimilation. Smaller meals and rest periods are sprinkled throughout the day. With this, we can view Volume control almost as a sort of dosing, with each block preparing the child for the next with an appropriately-loaded but not overwhelming amount of work. Working twice a day with rest allows the athlete to assimilate the physical load and information more efficiently, enhancing results. Athletes who train in a single block must be careful and are forced to lower the quality to support the workload of training.

An athlete must enjoy the process to increase the motivation and willingness to best cope with rigours of training. Unfortunately, as young athletes continue to develop, the stress levels they experience also increase. My suggestion to ease the pressure is a tried and tested method—game-based learning. Incorporating drills based on games engages students of all ages in the learning process. Through games, the students learn various skills, but most importantly, they have fun. It takes one good shot to bring the student back the next day. The more they enjoy, the more they practice and improve. The more they progress, the more they practice and so on. Volume accelerates the learning curve.

Volume is also about what things, big and small, can get the athlete to practice for as long as they need to. The right athletic clothing and equipment that can withstand the stress of constant use by young athletes is vital to keep them motivated and injury-free. Training has to be exciting. One way to motivate high achievers is by adding a grade of difficulty. It is important to present young students with a higher goal and make sure that we continually challenge them every time they reach one by giving them a new one.

Another thing that I have found is that an athlete needs to be able to choose their music to blast while practising. The courts at my academy are always a confusing sonic storm of genres, with each athlete playing what energizes them the most and keeps them engaged during practice— rock, pop, rap, merengue, salsa, reggaeton—music in all different languages and from all different cultures that assist the athlete in reaching the volume of practice they need. It is a beautiful thing to see.

Athletes must be involved in their process by having some autonomy over the controllable goals and personal bests. In addition, athletes must understand their bodies and how they assimilate instruction, workloads and work–rest ratio. Volume is one of the principles that I consider to be sacred. Training can be carried out thoroughly with what some call deep practice. Still, if there is not a sufficient workload of training hours, the results will not be optimal.

6
QUALITY

Masaaki Morita is the previous CEO of the Sony Corporation and founder of the Morita Foundation, an organization that specializes in finding tennis prodigies to boost Japan's national presence in the sport. I have had the wonderful opportunity to become friends and work alongside Morita over the last several years, especially in the training of Kei Nishikori, whose career was initially funded by the Morita Foundation.

Morita is a phenomenal storyteller and our professional partnership has afforded me the opportunity to learn a lot from the way he narrates his life stories. He started the Sony Corporation with his older brother just after the Second World War, when Japan was struggling with local industry in the wake of several major national defeats. Morita and his brother, Akio, had a dream about revolutionizing the way music was heard—a dream of portability and ease that they would later develop into the Walkman. The brothers realized their dream through their endless pursuit of Quality, constantly changing and improving to never rest on their laurels.

Quality is at the heart of all pursuits in elite sports; it is the cornerstone of all growth, development and skill.

A respect for Quality and the discipline to maintain that respect in training must be established at an early age, as it grows with the athlete.

As with all nuances of training, measuring an athlete's handle on any principle requires an intimate knowledge of the player. However, in the case of Quality, there is another layer of perspective that needs to be taken into consideration. Quality is a subjective idea that changes based on who is doing the evaluation. When we talk about implementing a spirit of 100 per cent effort into training, the only way a coach is going to be able to accurately measure how much of themselves the athlete is putting into even the most inconsequential seeming drill or exercise is by comparing it to past competitions. A good coach should establish attainable goals for the athlete to reach various baselines for their overall quality. This is what makes the pursuit of genuine Quality an ever-changing principle as comparisons to your past selves are inevitable, and so you are forced to try as hard as you can to not stagnate.

The subjective nature of the idea of Quality can seem too abstract to be helpful. So, to avoid further confusion, I will explain it as follows—Since Quality is all about consistency, **Routines** obviously play a huge part in the process. The best players are prepared ahead of time, not just with equipment and punctuality but with concrete goals of the day and genuine enthusiasm. This kind of motivation cannot, ultimately, come from their parents, their coaches or any member of their support team. Fostering this kind of motivation is entirely up to the athlete.

Because this kind of genuine motivation comes from inside the athlete, their **Discipline** must be ever-present and unbreakable. In the world of elite sports, there are no excuses or weak explanations for not bringing everything that you have got to every practice session. This is a matter of principle, yes, but it is also a matter of pragmatism. There just isn't enough time to waste on half-measures. There is no room to take a day off when you 'don't feel it'. You need to push through any fogginess, both mental and physical, and buckle down to get what you need to get done. The schedule is early morning workouts, school, more hard workouts, more school. And when the day is over, you proceed to rise again at the same ungodly hour to do it all over again, with an ever-escalating degree of intensity. This makes time management a huge component of discipline because the athlete needs to be operating at as close to 100 per cent efficiency as humanly possible in order to balance everything they need to do.

This sense of internalized discipline is also vital for an athlete's gameplay, since being able to focus and cut out all distraction is a crucial element of playing at a high level, and this is honed on and off the court.

Many athletes, musicians and writers, now world-renowned, did not achieve elite status until later in their careers. They are testament to the fact that discipline is central to success. The only way to reach the level of greatness that they eventually did is to push through the potentially overwhelming nature of their grind to the top and still consistently bring everything to every practice and event, never giving up.

Concentration is a component of discipline but it is also very much its own thing. When we hear talk of people showing incredible 'mental toughness', this is what they are referring to. Concentration is the ability to keep your mind zeroed in on one thing and to not let it get hung up on any distractions. Having your mind drift away by entertaining harmful and irrelevant thoughts is the number one way to ruin an athlete's mental game. Think of a Formula 1 driver. They have to maintain their concentration throughout the race, maintaining tactical planning and strategy for the hour and a half that the competition lasts. And it does not do them any good if they do not have the mental fortitude to stick to anything but the race at hand, stay in the present and in the very difficult 'now'.

Many people will tell you this kind of mental exercise can only be achieved by a sports psychologist, but that is not true. All the athletes at my academy are forged in fire. During games between students, I often purposely disrupt the match to force the players to concentrate beyond what they normally would. I make erroneous calls; change the score so that the winning player is no longer ahead; make them play with a different racket than the one they are used to right in the middle of a set, etc. These games are not just for fun. We base the player's rankings at the academy on them. There are real stakes for everyone involved. I do not want to hear excuses or complaints. I only want to see these athletes buckle down and concentrate on making up for these setbacks.

A lot of people mix up **Focus** and concentration, which is somewhat understandable. The difference is fairly subtle but absolutely key. Concentration applies to an entire match or situation, whereas focus is an even more zoomed in version of that. It requires absolute full-body attention on specific actions, like that of a Formula 1 driver on long straight drives at 300 km per hour or when approaching a sharp turn. With that level of focus, an athlete can improve his chances of being 'in the zone'.

It is a cliché that gets used haphazardly whenever we see anyone on any kind of streak, but to be 'in the zone' as an athlete is far more rare and much more transformative. It is when their performance is flawless. They experience the match not as one whole to focus on but as a series of individual breaths and tiny muscle movements—each being focussed on with their entire being, each stitched together perfectly and each becoming so much more. The ball seems to move in slow motion. Nothing else matters.

In all my decades of sports coaching and with all the No. 1 players whom I have trained over that time, I can count the number of players who have genuinely experienced being 'in the zone' on one hand. It is exceptionally rare; the holy grail of sports endeavors. It is what we are all striving for, even if we never reach it. This means absolute commitment to absolute focus.

Absolute focus means, Quality at all times, even during breaks and rest periods. The rule at the academy is that no player can have their cell phone on the court. A promising young man thought he was exempt from this and pulled out his cell phone on the bench between rest periods. I rushed over to him, snatched the phone out of his hand and threw it in the nearest trash can. I thought, for a moment, that his mother would be upset at me for throwing her son's property in the garbage but she was just as mad as I was. He had already been warned once, so she and I demanded absolute focus from him since then. She understood that to maintain the quality of training, the value of concentration and focus was essential and she supported our strict standards. In the end, he got his cell phone back.

Honesty may seem like an esoteric concept to apply to conducting quality training but it is as vital as any other component. Being honest with yourself and others goes back to the idea that elite athletics has no shortcuts. You have to do everything possible to get what you want. In the words of New England Patriots coach Bill Belichick, honesty is the foundation of talent.

Another aspect of honesty is **self-responsibility**. It is a lesson that all athletes must learn eventually as part of their path to true maturity. The essential fact of becoming an elite athlete is that beyond all the coaching and all the support, the weight of success lies on the athlete and no one else. Self-responsibility means understanding that your destiny is in your hands. This means having to conquer a fear of losing, embracing your own potential to fail and minimizing it as much as possible.

The last component to developing quality training is **purpose**. An athlete having a clear understanding of the purpose behind the training is vital to foster the kind of internal motivation that is necessary to spur quality work. This goes back to periodization planning and establishing clear goals that work logically up to the player's loftiest goals. The athlete always needs context in order to stay motivated.

What Morita was trying to achieve, with both Sony and his tennis foundation, is not just Quality, but what the Japanese call 'kaizen', which roughly translates to 'change for the better' or 'constant improvement'. The goal is not just to reach your full potential but to constantly be able to tap into the potential in every aspect of your journey, over and over and over again, until it becomes second nature and you are able to tackle any and all obstacles in the best way possible.

7

REPETITION

When you see someone like Roger Federer in action, it is impossible to really imagine the level of hard work and difficulty that goes into every play, stroke and movement. This is partly because the effortless look makes the mechanics of any sport appear fairly opaque to anyone who has not trained in it on some level, but also because elite athleticism takes on a sort of accidental beauty that is stunning in how natural it seems, despite the infinite sea of effort that we know, if not experientially then intellectually, goes into making it look so easy. David Foster Wallace, a writer whose essays on tennis are some of the best in the genre, described this kind of spectacle in his *New York Times* article 'Roger Federer as Religious Experience': 'The human beauty we're talking about here is beauty of a particular type; it might be called kinetic beauty. Its power and appeal are universal. It has nothing to do with sex or cultural norms. What it seems to have to do with, really, is human beings' reconciliation with the fact of having a body.'[4]

---

[4]Foster Wallace, David, 'Roger Federer as Religious Experience', *The New York Times*, 20 August 2006, https://nyti.ms/2KCpqQT. Accessed on 9 February 2023.

I've spoken quite a lot about Repetition so far in this book, but the principle is worth exploring in slightly more detail, because repetition is, unsurprisingly, the cornerstone of training, and thus of elite athleticism in general.

I'm sure we've all heard the age-old bromide 'practice makes perfect'. Like all of these kinds of platitudes, there is a kind of universal and transcendent truth to this that we often fail to recognize through, ironically, the phrase's sheer repetition. People are always looking for shortcuts and miracles, trying to get to an exceptional place without doing the work that is required to get there. This urge goes back to our conversation about talent—it is easier, on a general level, for people to accept God-given ability and unblemished natural expertise than to face the incredibly strenuous and taxing realities of elite sports training. No matter how hard we try, we can never escape that fundamental truth, immovable and sometimes mean, like gravity—practice makes perfect because putting in the time is the only way to get better.

Repetition is the easiest and fastest way to learn; it relies not just on making the motion, but understanding, breaking down and performing the mechanics behind the movement. Athletes often need footage of their work as concrete feedback to establish this understanding. Then, when it is all set and done, it becomes about the number of copies that you can duplicate and how true they stay to the original.

A good example from tennis is Pete Sampras working on his serve. His routine was the same every day—after dinner, he would go down to the same court and, after a quick shoulder warm-up, he'd place a ball out wide on the deuce court and proceed to practice his serve, aiming for that particular spot. If he managed to hit the ball, he would replace it and continue. He never practised any other shot during this time, or any other kind of serve; he intended on mastering his wide serve to the deuce court. He practised over and over and over again, 30 minutes every day devoted to this one thing, for days and months and years. When I would go down to the court to see how he was doing, he would often try to bet $100 on his ability to hit his target. At first, I thought he was trying to put pressure on himself in order to get it right, but realized he was too good to lose and made the bet so expensive to drive me away from his practices. He never wanted anyone on the sidelines of this part of his training.

Monica Seles is another example of a player who integrated Repetition into their training more than almost anyone else. She was a perfectionist, able to keep doing the same motion over and over again beyond the comprehension of anyone else. She was like a robot, completely and utterly unstoppable. At one point, we had three people serving against her so she could practice returning. She would return all their serves, over and over again. It reached a point where all 3 of her opponents' shoulders gave out, injured through repeated use, but Monica kept going.

It should be noted that these exercises are fairly linear in their nature, i.e., the mechanics to achieve the motion never evolves past a certain point. It is important to remember that Repetition is not the same as stagnation. Doing the same thing over and over again is key to progress, but like with all exercises and training programmes, you should be able to adapt and change to the athlete's needs.

For example, my brother, Jorge, was no stranger to repetition, since swimming, more than most sports, requires endless practice. He had done hundreds or even thousands of hours of laps in his lifetime, constantly training for major competitions. However, he and his team knew that, with Jorge being 5 ft and 8 in. (relatively short for a swimmer), he was more likely to lose fractions of seconds off blocks and turns than anywhere else. So, a new repetition-based exercise was established for him to work on every day after practice. He was to practice taking off the block and swimming a few strokes before getting out and doing it again, The second part of this training was to stand at the height of the flags, about 5 m away, and to swim quickly to the wall to practice the turns. Jorge told me when he explained the whole process, 'If you want something that much, it has to cost you that much.'

Perhaps the greatest endorsement of the benefit of repetition comes from my time with one of the greatest players of all time. When he was at the academy, Agassi and I would carve out an hour, from noon to 1 p.m., to work on his strength and racket speed. I would feed him balls over and over and over again, every day for weeks and months and years. Almost everyone I talked to at that point did not believe in what I was doing. They told me I would ruin his shoulder by making him do this on top of his normal practice hours. They were wrong. Not only did this special training give Agassi the strength and speed that he eventually used to reach the heights that he did, but there was an unforeseen benefit, one that became a key component of his success.

This Repetition essentially allowed him to invent a new

type of stroke—the swinging volley. A powerful offensive option where he could hit both forehand and backhand and which, combined with his already aggressive style of play focussed on playing close to the baseline, gave his opponent virtually no time to breathe. This shot helped him do well in tournaments and became such a staple of his game that it changed the way he played competitive tennis as a whole. This stroke, along with other aspects of his style of play, was copied by virtually everyone. Hitting this type of volley became mandatory for other players. Today, such a move is expected and essential in every player's arsenal. That kind of impact was not our intention but is the result of the power of repetition, continued grind and always striving to get better.

When I was training Agassi and beginning to realize the magnitude of this development, I reflected on what brought us to this point—hours and hours of training when everyone else was off doing other things. The courts were empty. The air hummed. I took stock of every detail—the warmth of the court rising up, the gentle breeze of the wind against our sweaty faces and the rhythmic puck of every ball Agassi hit. I realized I had been here before and had felt this kind of feeling before. When Jorge practised his takeoffs and his turns, it was always after hours. It used to be cold and dark outside and he was the only swimmer in that huge Olympic pool with the strong chlorine smell, the low flying bats, the twinkling of lights on the mountain and the echoing of every splash. It would always just be Jorge, my mom training him and me, sitting along on the bleachers for moral support. My brother's practice would cause the water to splash in the same ways, over and over again, with similar waves being made every time and breaking the silence of the quiet night. This kind of intense practice isn't sexy or sensational but it is deeply necessary for the development of talent and skill.

In this way, high-performance sports are like a Swiss watch—complicated, driven by precision with many parts being handmade and engineered to work together in harmony. The mechanics of any sport are the same. We must work on each part, honing and refining it until we can replicate it perfectly, all with the ultimate goal of processing every physical and cognitive skill automatically in an integrated way. Solid and nuanced repetition is the first step to be taken.

SECTION III

TRAINING NUANCES

8

VARIATION

When I first arrived at Nick Bollettieri's Tennis Academy (NBTA), he had the students doing the same repetitive drills over and over again. As I have said, repetition is key, but the training regime was too stagnant to really help anybody. Talented young players used to constantly talk back, calling the drills a waste of time. And they were right—we had to completely revamp the programme's training with a new athletic philosophy; one that focussed on the benefits of variation.

For a good analogy, we should cast our minds back to the days of our early adulthood, when we first had to fend for ourselves and live on our own. Cooking three meals a day every day while trying to stay within your budget and maintaining some semblance of nutritional value is difficult for anyone when they start making their own food. What ends up happening is that we fall into a kind of a routine. We have a handful of quick and easy recipes in our backpack that we return to again and again. This might work for a while, might even keep us healthy and financially responsible, but preparing the same 3 or 4 meals gets boring after a while and we also don't develop our cooking skills because we are not challenging ourselves. In order to do that, we have to introduce variation. Maybe you try out a new recipe that you saw online, or you try to spice up one of your signature dishes with new ingredients or preparation measures. As you continue to branch out, you get better at cooking, which inevitably makes you more comfortable and thus more willing to try new things. This process of change and variety is the only way to truly broaden your horizons and improve your skills in order to break your plateaus.

It can be hard to engage in this process, though, because it is much more difficult overall. You have to be willing to try new things and fail in order to get better. It is also less immediately satisfying. If you just do the same thing over and over again, you can see marked improvement because what you are comparing yourself to is obvious and ingrained in you. The process of developing muscle memory for a sport, say, is more boring but can feel more rewarding, since your strides are very linear and clear. But again, even though repetition is key, there are also three components to training that need to be taken into account equally—Repetition, Volume and Variety. They are, in the most basic terms, the act of doing something over and over again, how much you do that thing over and over again and what thing you are doing over and over again.

Here's another analogy: think of a young business associate who is just starting out. They have bought maybe one or two ties for the job and have learnt a simple knot in order to look professional. This is their entire arsenal, and so, this is the tie and the knot they use for every occasion. As they work for longer, they not only get better at tying a tie, but they might also get news one as gifts from a family member during the holidays or a congratulatory gesture for a promotion. They might just buy more ties now that they are making more money because they understand the importance of having a bigger arsenal and of having options. At some point, the act of tying a tie becomes automatic, and so, they might even learn new knots to further customize their look. They now have the chance to coordinate outfits, pick colors and patterns for different occasions. We can see how all these principles work together in this person's aesthetic growth—Repetition of action is aided by Volume, which leads to Variation; Variation boosts Volume via Repetition, and so on. These things are intimately connected and you cannot neglect any of them without the others suffering.

Jorge knew the dangers of stagnation very well. He was always able to know exactly when he had hit a plateau because of his timings and he was able to swim 15 m to 50 m sprints, butterfly style and all, consistently in 32 seconds. To improve, he added Variation to every aspect of his training. His rest times, distances and sprint numbers changed. He did this in order to shock his body out of a pattern and to disrupt his sense of complacency. It always worked.

With this change though, it is important to note the ways in which the shakeup occurred. It is still vital that the athlete do things that are directly related to the sport they are training in since the ultimate goal is to build muscle memory and improve a certain set of skills. Obviously, it does not make sense for Jorge to start running or lifting weights to break through his plateau, that is variety, but it is not relevant to what he is trying to do. Too much variety can make it so that a player never learns anything and never gets better, just like too much repetition can do the same.

Variation has to be more subtle and intricate than that. This also applies to the number of drills and exercises, not just which ones get chosen. Having a player do too many different drills only confuses them and spreads them too thin. Again, Variation is all about finding a balance between the old and the new, between what works now and what will work to create a better future.

To implement the Variation correctly, the coach needs to select the part that needs work. Then, you track and monitor how the athletes **respond** to this change from this point forward. If it negatively affects their game, then you select something else. This part of the process can, in many ways, be like a computer scientist altering and writing code. If you change too many things at once and something goes wrong, you will not know what exactly is giving your athlete trouble. Therefore, you want to be systematic in how you approach the Variation. Once you observe how the athlete responds to the interpretation, fully implement the change into their programme and watch their game **mutate** and develop in response. Eventually, the player **evolves** and grows in their skills with enough proper variation. In short, select, respond, mutate and evolve.

An organic difficulty curve must be created and respected for an athlete to evolve naturally. You want to establish a nice clean ramp-up to the more complex stuff instead of exhausting your player or lulling them into a false sense of confidence with easy exercises that may lead to severe injuries to the body and ego later on. Starting at a high pace and never lightening up severely disparages or hurts an athlete. On the other hand, constructing a difficulty curve that is too easy with inappropriate spikes in Intensity is like running into a brick wall when it's mapped out and has a similar effect on the athlete. Creating a dynamic and effective learning curve is difficult because you always have to be pushing the athlete while being careful not to run them ragged. Removing the comfort zone is key. Always have an athlete operate beyond what they are comfortable with, constantly moving that marker further and further beyond. By doing this, you are constantly pushing the athlete beyond their limits, but in a way that is gradual, like stretching. This forces the athlete to meet this new normal every time they do the exercise and helps them constantly improve. The body begins to anticipate the upcoming increase in intensity, which raises the player's overall fitness and performance. This phenomenon is called the supercompensation effect.

It is worth pointing out that an athlete might invite a more intense challenge to prove themselves, especially hot-headed young boys, but it is your job as a coach to know what is best for them and to train them accordingly, even if they don't understand it and think they know better. This is not to say there should be no communication at all, but do not entertain blatantly bad ideas. Once, when Jorge was trying to work on his lung capacity, he began swimming underwater, for 25 m at first, then for 50 m and then finally for 100 m stretches. His coach had him do one more at 100 m and Jorge went to the emergency room trying to prove his abilities by going past the mark. This kind of thing, of course, is never a good idea, even without the immediate threat of drowning.

At the end of most workouts, the athlete should still have energy reserves. He should feel like he could keep going a little longer. However, at other times, we should push the player to the max, beyond their comfort zone. These variations do not allow adaptation and constantly force the athlete to improve in their learning zone.

There are generally different types of Variation, all acting at different levels of gameplay. The most advanced Variation allows the player to grow and develop tactical strategies and stress-relieving mechanisms. Doing something better than others does not matter if you do not know when and how to implement that thing into your game correctly. This kind of Variation is intuitive. It only makes sense that a player who has played more matches, been up against more opponents and has operated in more environments has a higher level of knowledge and performance, just by their sheer experience. This is also one of the benefits of getting a player into a high-level training programme when they're young. They start to build up experience earlier and have access to all of the knowledge of the staff as well.

Tactical knowledge is a huge part of Variation, even on the micro levels, because Variation is, ultimately, about adaptation. Another kind of training that can be helpful in this regard is what has become a recreational staple at many institutions, which is to allow the students to play against one another without the staff present, purely on their own desire for fun competition. The change in context allows the athletes to play in a way that they normally would not and it is a kind of natural Variation that can positively influence their gameplay over time by forcing them to use their arsenal of skills in new ways.

This can also be a way for athletes prone to perfectionism to relax and not take their training so seriously. Perfectionism is a trap that many budding athletes never manage to get out of. Trying to conceive an ideal version of every movement, stroke and play, and then doing that every single time, is not only impossible but also makes it harder for the player to adapt their tactics. They lock up and get obsessed with avoiding failure, not realizing that failure is part of the process. The more casual atmosphere of unmonitored friendly games is less tense and can be a step toward shaking some of those bad habits. It is itself a kind of Variation.

When it comes to what specific drills to implement in order to change up an athlete's training schedule, that question can only be answered on a case-by-case basis. What I will say, however, is that like with any other aspects of coaching, the best coaches listen and learn from their peers and take advice from the best in the field. Keep in mind, this goes beyond just what exercises to choose from but also speaks to the larger realm of philosophy. I cannot tell you how often I have gone to high-end coaching conferences or taken coaching courses where the primary concern of most people was to find out new drills for their players as if a certain number of different exercises and more reps was the key to superstardom. It is not that those questions are unnecessary, but that they are of the lowest possible concern regarding what it takes to make a champion.

Variation is the final key to an effective training programme. It is all about flexibility and knowing what needs to be addressed. The best coaches are the ones who are able to challenge and encourage their players in new ways; and the best athletes are always the ones who are able to meet that challenge head-on. Our job is to stretch them more every time without breaking them.

9

SPECIFICITY

Similar to how I spoke about routine in the last chapter, there are nuances to specificity that rarely get discussed. I am, once again, not just referring to the process of creating a specialized training programme or understanding what makes your athlete tick, but about the process of actually breaking down and disseminating each aspect of every component of your athlete's gameplay.

As a principle, specificity is all about organizing increasingly narrow goals in order to improve on aspects of your gameplay that would not get directly worked on. This is another instance where intimate knowledge of your players and a genuine and honest connection with them is absolutely vital.

It is not realistic to only work on one thing at a time since there is no space in an elite athlete's schedule for that kind of slow pace. So, beyond working in drills and exercises that incorporate multiple components, you can also implement what I call 'special help' sessions with players—a half hour time slot after practice for them to hone one aspect of their game that they think they need to improve.

A lot of the specificity comes down to players being able to analyse their own game, identify what we call weapons and weaknesses and work on those things themselves. For example, a golfer may say his best shot is with the 7-iron, but he needs to be encouraged to dig deeper. What 7-iron? What distance? What about the slice? The hook? Upwind? Downwind? Uphill? Downhill? Coaches must teach players not to think of the game or their skills in terms of monolithic ideas. As Tiger Woods once said, 'No matter how good you get, you can always get better, and that's the exciting part.'[5] Elite athletes can plumb the absolute depths of their game to improve constantly.

As I mentioned in a previous chapter, the decision to improve a weakness or develop a weapon can only be answered case-by-case. However, we must admit that a strong weapon tends to be more problematic for an athlete's opponent than the absence of weaknesses. Therefore, it all depends on your athlete's specific style of play and what he wants to improve. Also, keep in mind that what you choose to specify in your training can be as straightforward or as complicated as you need it to be, from a simple stroke to a specific situation.

Let's look at Pete Sampras and Andre Agassi again, to compare their very different approaches to a fundamental aspect of their game—the serve. Agassi's philosophy was always that you are only ever as good as your second serve, i.e., he never wanted to be in a position where he was caught out for whatever reason (stress, anxiety, exhaustion, etc.) and had to resort to a weak second serve. He practised his second serve to the point where it became so reliable

[5]'7 Best Tiger Woods Quotes to Achieve Greatness', *Tiger Woods News*, 27 December 2021, https://bit.ly/3lmmP4v. Accessed on 9 February 2023.

that he was able to experiment with certain risky shots on the first serve without fear of double faulting. This tied into his larger goals with regards to training. Everything, from how many balls he kept in play to how consistently he was able to hit a target, was measured and improved in the subsequent practice. His training was all about critical decision-making and tactical manoeuvers, all framed with data and numbers.

Sampras, on the other hand, had a more fundamentals-based training philosophy, the goal being to ingrain muscle memory within him to the point where he was able to think and move faster based on what he did not have to consider. Sampras's approach to serving was the reverse of Agassi's—if you make your first serve so that it works for you every time, then there's no need to worry about a second serve at all. And you can see, in the way they both approached their training and the serve, how these different approaches worked specifically for both of them and fuelled their respective styles of play.

There is one other factor to this difference that is crucial to keep in mind—because specificity and periodization are two sides of the same coin (or, maybe more accurately, different levels of details on the same side of a coin), athletes with radically different approaches like this should never practise together. They can obviously play against one another, especially if they are some of the best competition that the others have access to in their pool of consistent peers, but muddling what works best for them will only ever hurt their improvement process and waste their time. Agassi and Sampras never practised together but they did not even practise with other players of their skill level. Those talented athletes took the opportunity to train with others of lower skill and sparring partners to work specifically on their unique needs. Every second of training was focussed on developing every part of their games. Two players of equal talent waste time practising together since the work has to be divided to meet the specific needs of each of them. Parents and coaches should remember that it is essential that each player's unique needs are respected and accommodated to reach their full potential.

Specificity is all about knowing your players and having them play an active role in diagnosing and developing their gameplay. But in order to do that and to ensure that they can achieve their dreams, they have to dig deep down into themselves and their tendencies to develop themselves and constantly improve.

10

COMPETITION

An obvious yet somewhat overlooked component of the development of an elite athlete is the nature of competition itself. It should go without saying that becoming the best in the world does not involve some esoteric debate about the merits of various athletes' play styles. Rather, being the best is a matter of objective and mathematical fact based on agreed-upon organizational rankings. The logic of competition is fairly straightforward—you train hard in order to get better at the game in order to win more matches in order to place higher in tournaments in order to increase your ranking in order to get closer and closer to being world No. 1 until you finally make it there. Why am I bothering to outline something so self-evident? Because re-evaluating what we take for granted is an invaluable element of the philosophy behind elite athletic training.

Contrary to popular belief, there is no scientific consensus on whether competitiveness is an innate biological quality in human beings. There is a lot of theory, especially stemming from Sigmund Freud and psychoanalysis, that would say competition is intrinsic to humans, and a lot of people would cite Charles Darwin's 'survival of the fittest' idea as further proof, but not only is the concept of competition as the best method of survival not to be found anywhere in Darwin's seminal book *On the Origin of Species* (in fact, 'survival of the fittest' is an over-simplified colloquialism that Darwin never used), but his theory of evolution revolved around the idea of adaptation, or the lack thereof, in response to environmental precedents, not direct competition between species. There is just as much theory that says the enthusiasm for competition is a deeply ingrained social construct, coming more from the way the tent poles of capitalism, namely the so-called 'free market' and the by-the-bootstraps idealization of hard work, bleed into our everyday lives.

I bring up this disparity because, regardless of what the case may actually be, the world of elite athleticism is inherently competitive. Competition is the foundational context of all sports. Tennis, golf, swimming, football and everything else are zero-sum games, meaning that winning them is only possible if other people lose. There is a tendency in sports today for parents to want to take an 'everybody wins' approach to these games, giving everyone participation trophies and showering them with praise simply for showing up and playing. While this approach, similar to the 'all-rounder' conception of sports scheduling we discussed in an earlier chapter, may have some merits for parents using sports simply for their child's social and physical development, this is totally and completely antithetical to the entire idea of elite athleticism.

This is why I insist on teaching young players the rules of the sport as early as possible; it is all about establishing the proper context for the athletes to get used to. Rules provide framework, which provides stakes for drills and other more abstract types of practice. Rules matter. Points matter. Strategy matters. This is also why I demand that parents have an intimate knowledge of the rules of the sport that their child is participating in, since the context the competition provides exists both on and off the court.

The competition training block is perhaps one of the most important. In the end, what matters are the results. A parent–coach role is vital; this is where the children learn to fight, to not surrender and to try until the last moment. These characteristics that many sports heroes have—Tiger Woods, Peyton Manning, Mia Hamm, Serena Williams, Rafael Nadal and more—all formed their competitive character from an early age with the help of their parents.

Parents who help their children from the beginning understand the importance of competition and encourage them to compete without putting pressure on them about results. This way, their children learn to win but also to lose. The only accurate way to measure an athlete's evolution, in its entire context—movement mechanics, strategy/tactics and psychology—is under the pressure of competition. The more the athletes compete, the more experience they accumulate to help them confront the opponents and themselves.

Young male athletes tend to be more naturally competitive, whereas young female athletes tend to be more reserved, initially more unwilling to compete to the degree that they must. In Section III of this book, I have dedicated an entire chapter to the differences between male and female athletes brought on by various forms of socialization, and while this, of course, does not apply to every single athlete, it has tended to be the case throughout my decades of experience. When they first start on their journeys, young female athletes must be introduced to the world of high competition more gradually because they are socialized to be defined by their knack for cooperation, whereas young male athletes tend to have the opposite problem: their socialization leads them to be too gung ho for competition, which needs to be reigned in so they get perspective on what the true point of competition is—beyond winning and losing.

That point, coincidentally, has a lot to do with something that I mentioned a few chapters ago about the acquisition of knowledge. The stakes that competition introduce act learning opportunities for an athlete, regardless of the result of an event. It is vital, especially in the early stages, that the athlete stays focussed not so much on winning to the exclusion of everything else, but on developing healthy coping mechanisms for competitive pressure and developing their tactical sense beyond what they would be able to if they just win without any resistance repeatedly. It is up to the coach to help them get everything they can out of every experience, good and bad.

When I say that the spirit of competition exists off the court, I am not talking about some vague sense of rankings or mindset. For example, a previous athlete of ours, Tommy Haas, who was world No. 2 in 2002, made everything into a game. He loved to compete and had a child's eagerness when it came to all kinds of contests. When we would travel to events, we would always fly coach, which meant that we would always have a lot of time to kill at the gates of various airports. We developed a game to play while we waited, one that involved throwing a coin about 3 m away and seeing who could get closest to the wall without actually touching it.

Everyone we travelled with would always become enthralled with our silly exercise. Heated competitions would ensue with cheers and screams of excitement echoing after every masterful play. We would only stop when security was called, but the games wouldn't end there. We would always play something on these trips—cards, craps, backgammon, etc. We would make our own fun—racing to and from taxis and making the last one to arrive pay. Even when we reached the hotel, the games did not stop.

This might seem juvenile to some but it helped stoke the competitive energy needed to stay in the zone during the kind of high-stakes matches that these athletes partake in on the court. Finding a way to make competition central to every aspect of an athlete's life while also making it about genuine growth and learning is vital, and that process starts early on. The people who would not play the games that Nick and I set up, or who would try once or twice, lose and quit, lacked the tenacity to really be able to put that kind of competitive spirit into play at all, let alone find a healthy way to channel it throughout their lives. None of them ever went pro.

◆

At the heart of all competition is a struggle to balance two essential facets of play—attack and defence; or knowing when to take risks and when to fall back and wait for another opening. What to do when is, of course, an immensely complicated question that varies not just from person-to-person, but opponent-to-opponent, tournament-to-tournament and even from point-to-point. Knowing which side of the spectrum to lean onto and how hard is all about reading an ever-changing situation and piecing together a whole host of factors: How much longer do I expect to play this match? Am I ahead or behind? How does my play style fare on a moment-to-moment basis against my opponents'? Are they starting to panic, slip up and get nervous? Am I? What have I done up until this point in the game and what is it that they expect me to do?

José Mourinho, the best soccer coach of all time, describes how he is very aware of the tempo of the match. When the opposite team's fans get dumbed down, it is the time to take risks and attack. All this and so much more plays out at every micro-intersection of the game. A lot of this decision-making becomes second nature to coaches over time, but until that point, there are a few principles to keep in mind throughout a competition.

Firstly, those who do not take risks never get anywhere. Stagnation is mainly caused by complacency and comfort. And fear is the ultimate talent killer. As the old cliché goes, it is always better to regret doing something than regret not doing it. Successful athletes understand the importance of risk and reward. They would always rather go for a shot or a point or a tactic and fail than not go for said opportunity and fail in another way. You have to be willing to make mistakes, to push yourself and learn from your failures. You have to learn where your tendencies lie and work to counteract them: Do you clam up too often or do you constantly go for shots that put you out of position?

Perhaps the best example of a prolific risk-taker in high-ranking tennis is Gaël Monfils, a French player who, at the time of writing this, is ranked world No. 9 in the ATP (Association of Tennis Professionals) despite never having won any grand slams. He is possibly the most athletic tennis player ever to acquire this level of mainstream success. He is constantly diving, sliding and jumping around the court, going for impossible shots and saving impossible balls. He will return shots with his back to his opponent, balanced on the insides of his feet as he slides into a wide triangle or extend fully horizontal in order to keep a rally going, if only for another hit. Monfils has arguably the best, most exhilarating highlight reel in the entire modern game. In a 2017 profile on him for *The New York Times*, Ben Austen compares his feats to that of Keanu Reeves in *The Matrix*.[6]

This kind of prowess is only really possible because Monfils is a textbook risk-taker. He is ready and more than willing to go for the shots that other athletes would call impossible returns, using his elasticity to cover the court in an unprecedented way. This willingness to take risks can be, at times, more of a bug than a feature with regards to the success of his game. Monfils does not win as often as someone of his skill level should. If you break down the details of his career, the story becomes clear. His flashy athletics make him prone to want a dramatic show rather than a clean match, meaning that he wastes time and energy giving people a good performance in the early rounds of tournaments instead of saving himself for tougher, meatier opponents later on. This is unfortunate, but in a lot of ways, it is preferred to a more passive play style. It is always easier

---

[6]Austen, Ben, 'Gaël Monfils Hits Miraculous Shots. Why Can't He Win?', *The New York Times*, 24 August 2017, https://www.nytimes.com/interactive/2017/08/24/magazine/usopen-monfils-miraculous-shots.html. Accessed on 9 February, 2023.

for a coach to guide a player to manage these aggressive tendencies than to make a player with a passive style of play become more aggressive.

My favourite clip of Monfils is not any of the insane points that he is famous for, but actually a moment where he fails. In a match against John Isner, Monfils overextended to return a shot in the back-right corner; Isner seized this opportunity and answered with a simple drop shot, almost flippant and dismissive in how close it was to the net. Monfils took off running after it; we could see it in his movements that he believed he could do it, that he could still make it to the ball before the second bounce. Monfils ran and leaned at a 45° angle to the ground, his actions almost more like a graceful stumble than anything else; until the last second he did not reach out. He did all the calculation in his head in the span of just a few short seconds and it all came back to the same reality—he probably could have returned the ball but he would only be delaying the inevitable. He could not have stopped his momentum, so he would been even more out of position for the next shot and so on. Coming this hard and this fast at a ball is more likely to end up in an injury than a inning point. This was the right call. As everyone applauded Isner for the point and Monfils was unable to stop, he jumped over the net's camera stand, tucking his heels under him and clearing the whole setup by several inches. The commentators laughed and applauded his hurdling skills while the camera replayed the jump in slow motion. This moment encapsulated everything that is brilliant about Monfils's risk-taking and commitment to every point. It does not matter whether or not he won the rally, but that he was constantly putting himself out there while also doing all the split-second decision-making that is so vital to elite athletic success. The result is secondary to what the formed habit means for his game.

Another tip to consider for competition is one that has been outlined in the chapter about knowledge, namely that strategy and tactics are an essential part of the process, even more so in the raw numbers behind physical abilities. Being able to break down an opponent, their weaknesses, their strengths, their tendencies and their techniques gives you more edge than any amount of blind training can. You have to know what to adapt to in order to adapt.

This idea is the source of another ancient bromide: 'Knowing is half the battle'. Sun Tzu's *The Art of War* is one of, if not, the most widely quoted and studied resources on the nature of competition and conflict. In it, he stresses the importance of this kind of intimate knowledge, outlining the consequences of gaps in these important areas. He wrote, 'If you know the enemy and know yourself, you need not fear the result of a hundred battles. If you know yourself but not the enemy, for every victory gained you will also suffer a defeat. If you know neither the enemy nor yourself, you will succumb in every battle.'[7] There are obvious and vast differences between war and sports, but this principle still applies to all forms of conflict, even with the added distance of hundreds of years. It especially applies to high-level competition. The best and most successful competitors are the ones who show mastery over not just what their opponents are prone to do but what they are prone to do and can adjust their

---

[7]Tzu, Sun, *The Art of War*, Capstone Publishing, 2010.

tactics in accordance with the changing context of the game in question.

Lastly, there is the pressure that can weigh on a competitor and interfere with and hamper their skills. The expectation to win, especially if the odds are not overwhelmingly in your favour, is hard for anyone to operate under, and all of this anxiety is multiplied exponentially, the higher up you go in the ranks. I talk about the mental side of elite athleticism in more detail later, but the point is that the context of competition must be reinforced and understood from the early stages of an athlete's career to help minimize the prolonged and physical stage fright that a lot of athletes get hung up on. For me, this does not mean only setting up practice within the context of real matches in the way I have already outlined but also encouraging the students at my academy to play for keeps in their own time. Even the casual, friendlier matches are ones that have stakes, both tactile and social. Athletes often wager chores, food, possessions and other physical assets on the games they played outside of practice. The players who are the best, or the players who can best reach their full potential under the constant pressure of competition, not only win those assets but also gain a degree of status among their peers. We always keep these practices in check so as to not allow students to make the losses too punishing, but it is a system that virtually everyone is involved in and is almost entirely self-made—an organic result of the student's drive. It is also, in many ways, self-regulating. Many students are close enough in skill, so one group of kids never stays on top for long and this constant shuffle not only keeps cockiness and arrogance in check but also ensures that people always compete to try and shake up the hierarchy.

But the main takeaway from this practice is the most invaluable—competition and the drive to succeed is at the heart of all athleticism and getting students to understand that and break it down into all its most helpful parts is another critical piece in building up elite athletes. Do not let the results get in the way. The focus is on growth and lessons that form lifelong habits, especially in the earliest stages of their careers.

11

KNOWLEDGE

Takeda Shingen was a Japanese military leader from the late Sengoku period. He is not only one of the most famous figures from this period but from the country's entire history, boasting an impressive number of successful conquests across various Japanese provinces. While his role in shaping the history of Japan is almost unparalleled, he is perhaps best known colloquially as being credited for saying, 'Knowledge is not power, it is only potential.'

This is another fundamental fact of my approach to coaching—gaining and seeking knowledge is only half the battle. Someone who is well versed in all the theory and strategy of a particular practice is never guaranteed to be able to actually implement said practice, let alone implement it well, since knowledge and its application are very different things.

But even this distinction has many more layers—a spectrum of nuance that needs to be addressed. Let us, for a moment, think about parenting. If someone who is about to have a baby wants to get better at dealing with children, there are a variety of options available to them. They could read books about what to expect and how to tackle common problems. They could look online for videos and articles and blog posts, which are sources of information that may not be in print. They could join a group of soon-to-be parents and talk through their anxieties. They could discuss things with their own parents or other parents whom they know. They might reflect on relevant experiences from their past—maybe they have been a teacher or a babysitter, or they have a niece or nephew that they have taken care of from time to time.

All of these things give different kinds of knowledge that vary in relevance and distance to the skills that are directly involved in raising a child. All of these sources are helpful in their own way; however, you would never call someone who has done all these things but not had a child a 'parent'. It is true that this knowledge will make them more equipped to handle a baby than the average person, but they still do not actually have the skills to get the job done. You could not even really call them knowledgeable about parenting, because all the information they have is preemptive and theoretical; the knowledge never evolves because the situation never evolves.

That is the point to all of this—knowledge is power only when it is applied and expanded upon. You may get tired of me saying this about everything, but it is no less true. Knowledge is not a static thing; it is constantly growing, changing and shifting, adding new levels to itself the more you learn and adapt. True knowledge is constant analysis and re-evaluation of real experience at every level of play. The difference between wisdom and knowledge is the application and non-application of said information, respectively. True knowledge is only gained through action, trial and error. At the end of the day, the only way to get better at something is to do it.

Since a coach's job is to not only share wisdom with their athletes but to also guide and shape how that wisdom is always being applied, it can be very tempting to become cocky and take all the credit for an athlete's success. It was a trap I fell into a lot in the early days of my career. As I travelled the professional circuit with elite athletes, racking up win after win, I felt invincible. I wore my arrogance on my sleeve, naively thinking that I had learnt all there was to coaching within a few short years and that I was now one of the best in the business. Nothing but time can teach you that there is always a tomorrow and there are always losses to be endured. It was a hard lesson to learn but one that was absolutely vital. True humility is inevitable and necessary to rebuild. This is one reason why so many people never grow beyond a certain threshold—they are scared to let things go and endure a painful reworking for their own greater good. Not only are the best coaches humble and willing to stay behind the scenes of an athlete's career (where they belong), but they also understand that victory is not guaranteed and that wisdom should be an active and consistent force in an athlete's life.

These same types of lessons need to be learnt by the players, just in a slightly different way. I once coached a cocky and hard-headed young athlete. He was talented but always seemed to get ahead of himself. He once asked me, considering that he was sure that he had the best swings in the academy and that everyone had complimented him on the fluidity of his movements, how long did I think it would take him to reach his goal of becoming a champion and turning pro? I thought about it for a second and told him the truth—10 years. He was surprised. He angrily replied that I was wrong and that he would get there sooner because he trained hard with many hours of solid Repetition. I looked at him and told him that, in that case, it would take 20 years.

He liked that answer even less. It took me a while to explain that he did not understand the game even though he had great strokes. Finally, he looked thoughtful but agreed. That student's attitude still had a long way to go, but he realized that the only way to start getting positive results was to radically change the way he trained. Knowledge and experience allow us to deal with problematic students and to explain to them and convince them that we want to achieve their total well-being. And the students learn that it takes more than repetition to achieve success. By playing many practice matches and taking advantage of different circumstances, they are able to gain enough knowledge to put it into action when needed.

Another knowledge factor is context. This is partly to help motivate the player to learn how to think. The context provided by different game situations and real matches, even training sessions where you compete with low stress, is vital. Not only do you practice game mechanics but you also learn how to apply those moves in the context of competition. It also allows us to work on things within the mental sphere since point-to-point strategizing and game analysis can only happen within the evolving ecosystem of a real game. After every game, won or lost, the two things that you should ask your player and the two things that should always be at the front of their minds are: 'what did I learn from that match?' and 'how can I apply what I learnt to the next match?' Drills are essential, but they are not what the athlete is actually training for. Games are knowledge in action. Once again, the only way to get better at something is to do it.

Of course, game knowledge is only one thing that a coach is expected to teach. Because elite athletes grow up with the sport in the intense training environment that is necessary to help them foster their talent, it is also up to the coach to instil wisdom via life lessons that can be applied off the court. These children are being coached and brought up into adulthood by you and this world of intense competition. One of our roles as mentors is to teach these young athletes the moral obligation they have not just to themselves but to everyone around them, whether it is their parents, coaches, teammates, rivals and, maybe most importantly, less experienced players. We are carving character, creating positive attitude, work ethic, discipline and respect that are going to be called upon time and again for success in their daily lives.

Once you've travelled, your eyes are open forever.

Because high performance sports are international events, learning about other cultures is a vital component of this process as well. When Dominique Van Boekel was 20 years old, in the early stages of her professional tennis career, she had the opportunity to travel to Nigeria to play in a tournament. The entire event was being played across only three courts, since they did not have the funding for a larger venue. During a break between sets, she leaned against one of the net posts and the post immediately buckled, breaking into two parts. Because the organizers did not have a replacement for the net, the entire tournament had to be played out on the remaining two courts, which slowed the process down to an excruciating crawl. It was a supremely embarrassing moment for Dominique, but this, along with the general living conditions of many people whom she saw while visiting the city, also put a lot of her own resources and experiences into perspective, allowing her to reassess all the things she had taken for granted.

This reevaluation of her position in the world goes beyond the typical racist and reductive 'be grateful because there are starving children in Africa' style of thinking that many people mistake for worldly wisdom, especially in the West. Nigeria is an incredibly complicated and layered country. It has a rich history of art, music and entertainment, as well as violence, rampant political corruption and colonial trauma. These adversities, combined with a sustained population boom and a wealth of both tapped and untapped natural resources, has led to Nigeria having one of the starkest wealth gaps of any country, developed or otherwise. As of 2018, nearly 87 million Nigerians lived in extreme poverty, which is over 40 per cent of the country's population. African reporter Yomi Kazeem calls Nigeria 'the poverty capital of the world'.[8] Dominique was able to see this first-hand, with the homeless and disenfranchised begging on the street for simple amenities like food and water, makeshift bivouacs made from scraps and trash bags and whole families slowly dying of untreated diseases.

But Nigeria, like every other non-western (especially African) country, is filled with so much more humanity and joy than people tend to ever see. It has an incredible amount of cultural diversity, being home to over 250 ethnic groups.

---

[8]Alex, Tam, 'It Belongs to Me! A Libertarian Analysis of Property Rights in Nigeria', *The Journal of Libertarian Studies*, 15 July 2021, https://bit.ly/3IapjvH. Accessed on 9 February 2023.

The arts are robust and thriving there. Nigerian musicians are paving the way for the new sound of the continent; the Nollywood film industry is one of the most dynamic and well-established film industries outside of the US; and Nigerian writers, like Chinua Achebe and Chimamanda Ngozi Adichie, have written some of the most important and heart-wrenching works of literary fiction ever, African or otherwise. The country is filled with beauty and life and Dominique was able to see that too—children laughing and playing with a soccer ball, people chatting and sharing stories on their ways to run errands, bustling markets under a gorgeous sky. Walt Whitman once famously said that he contained multitudes; not only is this true for every person on this planet but it is also true for their cultures, communities and homes. These are the kind of experiences that travelling the world as an athlete can afford you, the kind of appreciation and perspective that this life can give young people. However, coaches have to be willing to push their students to see these intricacies.

Here's another, less stratified example. After Kei Nishikori, one of my greatest prodigies, played his first wild card in an ATP event in Colombia, I told him we were going on a trip to visit a well-known architectural monument, which was considered to be a treasure of that region and was a place that had nothing to do with sports. We drove with little traffic and a nice view on both sides, and as we went along, all signs of civilization were left behind. Kei looked pleased but said nothing.

After driving for some time, we arrived at our destination. We stood in line in front of an entrance to a pitch-black tunnel carved into the side of a large mound. Kei was even more perplexed when he was handed a hard hat before going inside. He had no idea what was going on but he followed me without complaint, down hundreds of feet of uneven cave floor and past literal tons of rocks. We wandered down through the caverns, dark, dank and unavoidable, with the smell of sulfur hanging in the thick air, until we finally burst through, fresh into what almost felt like daylight—an illuminated beacon deep within the cave. The Salt Cathedral of Zipaquirá is an enormous underground Roman Catholic church with stunning blue lights and statues of angels buttressing the high ceiling. Kei was absolutely mesmerized. His face was priceless. He kept looking around, gasping and asking how it was even possible to build something like this. These moments of true inspiration, of horizons being widened and expectations shattered, are also what knowledge, and its application thereof, is all about.

12

COMMUNICATION

Because true wisdom is knowledge in action, this means that another core component to bestowing knowledge on a young athlete is communication. You must know how to communicate the information in an effective way in order for it to be implemented. There may not be a more impressive and teachable example of the power of effective communication than that of the life of Koko.

Born in 1971, Koko was a western lowland gorilla who lived in a research institute in California and was studied for over 45 years by Dr Francine Patterson. Since Koko had been just 1-year-old, Dr Patterson had talked to her using a combination of spoken English and American Sign Language, or ASL, in an attempt to measure the intelligence of apes as well as the exact nature of language and language acquisition. Koko was one of the smartest animals that the world had ever seen, if not the smartest. She was very intelligent when it came to physical tasks. The 1978 film that made her famous, *Koko: A Talking Gorilla*, shows her drinking out of a glass of water with a straw and refilling it as well as properly playing with a toy View-Master and replacing its slides when she got bored. Her emotional intelligence went beyond what many people thought was possible. By the end of her life, Koko understood both spoken English as well as over a thousand signs that she would combine in all kinds of complex ways. She could talk about the abstracts of signing through sign itself, even attempting to teach other gorillas some words. She would combine the terms that she knew to refer to things she did not know ('finger' and 'bracelet' to make 'finger-bracelet' when referring to a ring, for example) and she was even able to express her feelings through abstract concepts—things like 'death', 'good', 'happy' and 'fake'. She convinced the staff to allow her to adopt a kitten, which she named All Ball; and a few months later, when Koko found out that the cat had been hit by a car, she was totally distraught, repeatedly signing things like 'sad', 'bad', 'frown' and 'trouble'.

This may not seem particularly relevant when we are talking about elite athleticism, but I believe there is a lot to learn from the depth and complexity Koko was able to convey during her life. The most important takeaway is that effective communication relies on a foundation of non-condescension. Dr Patterson was Koko's caretaker but did not talk down to or baby her, especially as their relationship went on. She spoke to Koko the way a great teacher might speak to a child, seeing her students as smart and complex vessels of endless potential in need of support. You cannot constantly underestimate your students and expect them to be great or do great things. A truly good coach learns, through time and dynamic engagement, what exactly it is that they can expect from their players on an individual basis and how to push them past those limits. A coach has to genuinely believe in the project they set out to make a reality—the project of cooperative self-improvement.

The other main takeaway we can get from Koko's story

is that extraordinary potential can only be reached in a very specific supportive environment. Koko would have been just another gorilla if she had not been cared for and pushed in many ways. A successful training environment is one that is tailored to an athlete's strengths, weaknesses and tendencies, one that works to improve the athlete via playing the long game instead of focussing on short-term spurts of instant gratification, one that can be adapted and changed when it needs to. A safe space in the most nuanced and integral sense of the word.

Building this kind of environment and communication is difficult, and anyone who tells you otherwise has not been able to truly foster anything like it. Of course, there are many books that talk about the proper ways to build communication skills, and while I am sure those kinds of how-to guides can be useful in a broad sense, there are some specific tenets of communication that come with the inherent power dynamic between a parent–coach and an athlete that need to be explored.

The point about non-condescension leads to perhaps what might seem like an obvious part of the process, despite how often it is dismissed and misunderstood by so many coaches: Good communication is based on having a strong relationship with your athlete. This means you cannot rule over them like a tyrannical dictator; rather, you have to understand and work with them to foster an environment of mutual respect. This means that you have to be honest with the athlete about the world that they are trying to break into as well as about their faults and weaknesses. However brutal and unwelcome the athlete might think this kind of assessment, your honesty has to be constructive, existing to build up rather than to put down or punish an athlete's sense of self. Mutual respect also involves a lot of listening. Learning and growing, both as a parent–coach and as an athlete, is not a linear process. You have to be ready and willing to make mistakes and acknowledge that you might not have all the answers, which involves an actual back-and-forth dialogue with your young athlete. This is not to suggest that an athlete always knows what is best for them, far from it. I am simply saying that you have to be open and ready to receive what your athlete has to say in order for your communication to be anywhere near effective. No one wants to follow someone who clearly does not care about them or who only sees them as a means to an end. That kind of tense relationship with an athlete is a death sentence for their career, or at least for your involvement in it.

For the information to be clear and useful, it must be presented in a practical and timely manner. It is also crucial to know the athlete thoroughly. Most parents assume that they know their children well, but unfortunately, they make many elementary mistakes—counterproductive words, inappropriate comments and wrong timing—that break down their relationships with their children.

The smart parents with whom I have had the pleasure of working have been firm, honest and very positive with their children. Verbally, they continually emphasize values, such as discipline, perseverance, work capacity and fighting spirit. Their conversations are open, back-and-forth dialogues, where both children and parents gradually learnt from each other.

But I have also met parents who have destroyed the careers of highly talented, hard-working and disciplined athletes. Branding young athletes as talented, intelligent and champions is the worst thing that a parent can do as there will always be someone better than them, and if they are winning today, they will surely lose tomorrow. These young people end up playing with fear and not enjoying the sport.

Unfortunately, many times, parents make comments without meaning to or without thinking. Believing that the little ones are mentally strong, they tease them after a game, calling them 'chicken', for instance. These silly comments gradually devastate the player's competitive spirit and, at the same time, rob them of their dream. It is of utmost importance that parents understand that their words carry an intense feeling and are taken in a more personal way, unlike a coach who can say the same thing which can be interpreted in a more depersonalized way by the young athlete. Hence, the importance of parent–coaches measuring their words with great caution.

Parents' moral support is essential for a highly competitive athlete's hard and long career, and this begins with healthy, intelligent and open communication, which is based on listening with an impartial, observant and tolerant mind.

Listening also means that you need to develop an intimate understanding of your athlete's emotional nuances and how they differ across lines of culture, age, gender, etc. As trite as it might sound, you really do have to understand where each athlete is coming from in order to guide them to where you know they can go. People, especially when they are young and more prone to emotional volatility, process things differently. You have to be able to know what to expect, what you can get away with and what works for a student versus another.

For example, once, when Kei stepped out of line during practice, I assumed my 'sergeant' persona and began yelling at him. I got up in his personal space and was screaming so much that I could see my saliva hitting his face. This is a mode I normally never use since these kinds of extreme strategies end up doing more harm than good in the long run, but I knew Kei, and Kei knew me, and we both understood that no matter how wild my external show of emotion was, it was simply that—a show. It is important to know that how you implement various methods of communication are often just as important as what method you end up choosing. I did not start screaming out of nowhere. Kei had had a disrespectful and poor attitude since practice had started and this tough communication method was a tactic that was implemented after a steady ramp up that proved my regular go-to moves ineffective in this situation. Kei understood my internal motivations and did not take it personally. He understood that this was just one, admittedly tough, way of communicating to him what I needed him to know. An hour later, he came to my office and apologized for his inappropriate behavior.

This kind of reading between the lines is hard to do and is only really possible after a solid relationship has been established. The player has to trust and believe the coach for the coach to help them as much as they are able to, and this trust can only be gained over time. It is worth it to mention that not every coach is a good fit for every player.

You also have to be willing to change your way of communicating with your player. When Ivan Lendl was training Andy Murray, Lendl and Judy, Murray's mother, were trying to figure out a way to help Murray understand how to serve out wide. They tried explaining it to him in a dozen different ways but nothing seemed to click. Finally, Lendl decided to go out on the court, assume the position of a ball catcher and tell Murray to hit the ball into his hand. Murray landed 10 shots in a row and was finally able to understand what he needed to do.

Being mindful of what approaches you use also sometimes means sticking to what's working when it is going well, even if it may seem nonsensical or silly. One of the top 10 players whom I coached had the bad habit of pushing when she was nervous. She had one of the best backhands down the line that I have ever seen, but she never seemed to have faith in herself. It seemed like she always needed to be reminded of her skill in order for her to play more aggressively. Her father was not a native English speaker, so during games, in an attempt to spur her on, he'd yell, 'Kitchen! Kitchen!' over and over again. We soon realized that what he was actually trying to yell was 'Chicken! Chicken!'—to call his daughter out. Although he had the wrong term, he was never concerned with looks or specific words, as long as she knew what he meant, which she did. It became like a code for them, with 'kitchen' being an intimate shorthand way to address her conservative play style. Instructions will always be coded differently depending on who you are training but that is not what is important. What is important is that the back-and-forth is happening at all.

This mindfulness also applies to all the broader nuances of communication as a whole. The vast majority of human interaction is non-verbal, even in a standard conversation.

You need to be aware of the image you are putting out—what it is you may be unconsciously putting behind words with facial expressions, inflections and body language. Your support needs to live in these realms as well. As a coach, you also need to be aware of what all these non-verbal cues say when implemented by your student. They can help you gauge understanding, honesty, exasperation, distress, apathy, etc., even if they do not directly hint at these feelings when talking to you. This is what it means to be a truly deep listener. Like everything else about effective communication, this will come with time, devotion, trial and error.

On top of being their coach, it is also crucial to be aware of your player's relationship with the world around them and how they react to certain things. On one occasion, when Kei was just starting his professional career, he faced Andy Roddick. The match was tight and Andy, feeling the pressure, chose to intimidate his young rival by hurling a series of racist epithets and verbal insults throughout the match. I could tell it was getting to Kei, even though he did not say a word during the whole match. I spoke with the head referee, but nothing was done. After the match, in the locker room, Kei leaned his racket against the bench and snapped it in half with a powerful kick. He proceeded to do this with all 10 of his rackets, seething with cold anger, still not saying a word. Reporters were impressed that he had maintained his composure, and during the press conference, Kei told them that he had not understood a word that Roddick had said. This decision is very indicative of how Kei handles these kinds of stressful situations. Being aware of how much players can take and how they will handle things is essential to help them stay mentally healthy and avoid public repercussions.

This idea of the public consequences of communication failures applies to the players' composure and that of the coaches. Once, two of my players were playing a quarter-final match at Court Suzanne Lenglen at the Stade Roland Garros in Paris. The stadium was packed with over 10,000 people, and it was an incredibly close match. I had worked closely with both of them but I was coaching only one of them at that particular moment. During a crucial game, the attrition war was beginning to wear on the nerves of both players. In a momentary lapse of good judgment, I shouted to my player, 'Don't worry, you know she chokes.' It took a few seconds for the audience to realize what I had said, but once they did, all 10,000 of them immediately started booing me. I was embarrassed and shocked at myself and at what I had done. I had nowhere to hide. I had tried to help one player with my stupid comment but had hurt the other one in the process. You can never unsay something, and so, it is important to remember that communication, in all its forms, involves forethought and an understanding of the consequences of various approaches, both good and bad; and the proper use of these tools allow you to transfer knowledge to your players much more effectively.

13

MALE AND FEMALE ATHLETES

As we dive deeper into the nuances of building an effective training programme for your child, it is important for us to acknowledge how large a role the sex and gender of an athlete play in their development. This applies to obvious biological differences revolving around strength and windows of growth, something I spoke about in Chapter 1, but the difference between male and female athletes goes well beyond that kind of physiology.

Although they are often conflated on a colloquial level, there is a scientific difference between sex and gender. Sex refers to the makeup of chromosomes and other biological components that exist, outside of specific intersex cases, as a male/female binary, whereas gender refers to a spectrum of identities based on a variety of social and personal forces. When we talk about the process of training boys versus the process of training girls, the vast majority of what we are talking about outside of trainability windows is influenced less by biological facts and more by facts of socialization, what we as a culture and a society expect of boys and girls and how that impacts their performance.

In 1999, a paper was published by scientists Kay Bussey and Albert Bandura in *Psychological Review*. It was titled

'Social Cognitive Theory of Gender Development and Differentiation' and it outlined the history of socialization studies as they apply to gender roles and the influence thereof in young children. In their paper, Bussey and Bandura develop their own refined theory of gendered socialization based on this vast history, a theory '[...] that posits that, through cognitive processing of direct and vicarious experiences, children come to categorize themselves as girls or boys, gain substantial knowledge of gender attributes and roles, and extract rules as to what types of behavior are considered appropriate for their gender'.[9]

Unlike other ideas of gender socialization up to this point, Bussey and Bandura point out that the research does not suggest an inherently motivating factor to any given gender role or norm with the self-identity of an individual. They push back against that assumption, saying, 'Just as having a conception of one's own gender does not drive one to personify the stereotype it embraces, nor does the self-conception of gender necessarily create positive valuation of the attributes and roles traditionally associated with it.' They conclude that: 'Both the valuation of certain attributes and roles and the eagerness to adopt them are influenced by the value society places on them'.[10] Put simply, there is nothing inherently masculine or feminine about any particular habit or action and that the main driver of our understanding of gender and what makes different genders valuable, both on

---

[9]Bussey, Kay, and Albert Bandura, 'Social Cognitive Theory of Gender Development and Differentiation', *Psychological Review*, 1999, https://bit.ly/3JYjzGy. Accessed on 9 February 2023.
[10]Ibid.

a personal level and a communal level, is steeped mostly in societal norms and expectations.

I mention all of this because these expectations work their way into every aspect of our lives, and as people involved in professional athletic training, these expectations are doubly present and doubly insidious. There are, of course, differences that come into play when training male and female athletes, but there are a lot of false sexist platitudes that pass as legitimate advice and it is important to empower athletes and their support groups with real information.

I have outlined seven 'Cs'—key differences between male and female athletes that need to be addressed and understood properly in order to ensure the highest possible quality of training. These are not hard and fast traits that apply to every boy or every girl but they do tend to be the general case based on a myriad of factors.

Competition: On the whole, the girls whom I have trained tend to be more averse to competition than boys are. The drive to beat other people, to dominate in a competitive environment and to be the undisputed best at what they do through conflict and competition does not tend to come as naturally to young girls as it does to young boys, who are very eager to prove themselves in these areas. Like I mentioned earlier, this has less to do with some abstract genetic competitive trait and more to do with how girls are socialized differently in virtually every culture. They are taught to be more passive, submissive and compliant, raised to hone interpersonal skills and not focus on physical attributes that do not directly link to cultural beauty standards. This is why my experience with getting young female athletes to commit to competition, in as visceral a way as is needed for elite athleticism, has often been much more difficult. In many ways, it goes against what society has taught them to value about themselves.

Female athletes have considerable adversity to losing, so a lot of my training with them, especially in their early development stages, revolves around leaning into this universal fact. This distinction between wanting to win and not wanting to lose is obvious and very relevant most of the time. Still, it is a distinction that could offer an alternative way into the head and heart of a female athlete you may otherwise have a hard time communicating with.

The inverse is also true for male athletes as the trouble with boys and competition tends to be an overly competitive spirit that overlooks genuine growth for simple wins if not regulated and reined in properly. I explained this in the last section, but it is important to keep in mind that the world of high-level sports is one with its own context and values, one that is more in line with what we as a culture tend to already teach and encourage in boys.

I recommend that girls play against boys whenever possible. This not only gets rid of social peer pressure that can be the cause of timidity when it comes to competition but also forces the female athlete, who is, in these cases, almost always playing with someone physically stronger than them, to buckle down and rely on their strengths, moving and playing in ways they would not otherwise.

Young male players see the other boys involved in the programme with the same goals, not as rivals, but as members of a seal team. They become friends, support each other, and always push one another to be better. They concentrate more on playing matches and not on personal matters. This characteristic of being able to practise and compete with each other strengthens everyone. Young male athletes love competition, making high-performance places ideal for developing competition skills.

Choking: When they begin to make mistakes, boys tend to tense up in a way that makes them stay in the moment much longer than necessary while girls tend to want to leave a situation as quickly as possible. These can both be detrimental to an athlete's gameplay, so it's important to recognize the symptoms of these impulses. The girls whom I have trained over the years, for example, tend to overcompensate by over-hitting and have to rein themselves in to a more controlled pace, which is a much harder way to recover than the other way around.

Boys tend to push and not go for their shots, missing clear opportunities due to the tension within the match. They are inclined to rely upon, albeit unconsciously, on their mechanical dexterity while choking, constantly pushing the ball rather than hitting it and are afraid to take risks. We can see how conventional male socialization signals this behavior. The man is supposed to be the alpha—composed and incorruptible. Boys tend to try harder at these times, with patience, seeking to find their levels of aggressiveness again.

Confidence: In the broadest possible sense, girls tend to be less confident than boys. This applies to life outside of elite athletics but it has special ramifications in our field. The reasons for this should be fairly obvious. Not only is the world of high-stakes competitive sports usually less intuitive a context for young girls to be ingrained in (based on the layers of cultural socialization I mentioned earlier) but it is also a context that simultaneously involves and encourages traits in young girls that do not mesh with traditional beauty standards while also demanding those standards to be upheld for the sake of the audience. Even some of the best athletes in the world, like Monica Seles and Mia Hamm, were riddled with self-confidence issues related to their appearance—their weight, outfits, hair, grace and beauty while playing. These are things that boys just do not have to think about. These things should not matter, but they do to the larger culture; and so it adds another layer of consideration that can undermine girls' feelings of self-worth.

Boys, on the other hand, are socialized to project unwavering self-confidence, which almost certainly makes it easier to compete but is a different standard that comes with its own set of issues. Boys are much less likely to show their emotions and reach out when they need help, since they have been told that they should be strong and emotionless. This can contribute to mental fatigue as this projection is often simply a coping mechanism. These young boys have not had the time or space to properly mature and so they tend to pave over internal issues rather than deal with them directly, especially in the context of elite athleticism, where it is often assumed that there is no time for that sort of thing.

There are many people, especially in the world of traditional sports coaching, who would say that are simply more skilled than girls are, but as we have discussed, none of these tendencies are inherent to sex or gender and you have to consider broader trends of cultural socialization when making these kinds of statements. For instance, one of the reasons why boys are seen as more skillful is because they usually display a wider variety of strategies and shots than female athletes. In my experience, this is because male athletes are not hindered by cultural expectations to look good and be taken seriously the same way female athletes are, especially when they become teenagers and sex appeal becomes a part of audience reaction, a thing that is as unfortunate as it is common. Thus, boys are more able and more willing, to make fools of themselves in order to try and get better at more things. It all comes back to confidence and wider trends. It does not mean that female athletes cannot do these things; it is that they are not encouraged to experiment and are actively set up to play the role the world wants them to.

Criticism: Obviously, in order to improve, both male and female athletes need dynamic feedback. They need both constructive criticism and honest dissections of their failures. Girls tend to take negative feedback more to heart (again, we can see a trend of negative cultural socialization and how it informs this kind of reaction), while being more receptive to constructive criticism. We also have to know that when girls cry, it is not because they are weak; it is the way they express their anger and frustration. Boys tend to be somewhat of the opposite. They tend to be less interested and enthused by positive feedback and more willing to take direct critique of their failures. Again, this goes back to socialization. Boys are not taught to exercise or appreciate compassion and are expected to be able to be strong enough to stifle whatever emotional response they might naturally have.

Navigating these tendencies is absolutely key to proper training, as is an understanding of what feedback feels and sounds like coming from certain parties over others. It is vital that parents not get involved in the criticism of their children and that all feedback be given to the coach to then be delivered to the player. This is to save parent–child relationships, which I will get more into in another chapter.

Closeness: This area refers to how attentive and involved a coach has to be during practice on a moment-to-moment basis. It is essential to create a strong bond with the female athlete from the start. Female athletes need to know that the coach cares; we have to earn their trust. Coaches have to make them feel unique and important at all times. The athletes throughout their development stage require a careful and personalized level of attention. Maximizing ability in girls is more challenging. It takes passion, energy and acute attention to every little detail. Before starting practices, we have to be very observant; we need to take note of their nails, hair, clothing; it is a way to show that we care.

Boys tend not to care if you take advantage of a break to go to another court to give instruction to another student, but girls tend to be much more sensitive about that type of attention splitting. Once again, this has nothing to do with the athlete's skill level or some kind of biological urge for reassurance but has everything to do with girls generally being more social and being taught to flourish best in cooperative and intimate situations.

Boys will not mind that kind of multitasking from a coach (although, of course, they need your full attention too), but you should be giving undivided attention to all your female athletes in a slightly different way. Girls' routines tend to be more personalized and specialized to be more effective, more than your average athletes'; and this includes having a close relationship with their parents. Girls tend to keep being directly involved with their parents until they turn 18 whereas boys tend to strive for independence around 13 years of age. Exceptionally talented women's training has to be approached slightly differently. Talented girls demand individualized workouts, with specific personal goals and 100 per cent attention. Again, these are all general symptoms of ingrained socialization and shouldn't be treated as default dispositions of anybody's sex or gender.

Conditioning: Girls develop personal techniques from an early age of nine and they are reluctant to change the style once it feels good. That is why the proper technique is vital during the formative part of the learning process.

It should come as no surprise that boys and girls tend to learn in different ways. Boys tend to be visual learners, preferring to emulate actions that they see and adapt through trial and error, whereas girls tend to be more auditory learners. Girls tend to prefer to apply discussion and explanation to their practice rather than physical examples.

Depending on your style and past experiences, this cannot be easy to understand. I know that, for my part, I tend to have a sense of urgency where information is short, clear and precise, favouring tactile examples over extensive verbal communication. I have had to learn to adapt my style to the student if it is clear that they understand better by other means. For example, when I was working with a very talented player, she often seemed lost and confused by my instructions. Luckily, we had a good relationship so she felt comfortable enough to be honest with me. She said, 'You always seem to be in a hurry. Please, if you want, slow down and talk to me. Give me a fuller explanation; I can do it when I understand the exercise.' This was a great learning moment for me. She is knowledgeable and a tremendously deep thinker, constantly analysing and breaking down every facet of everything she is given. I spent far more time talking to her during her training than with almost any other student I have ever had, going over the purpose and nuances of specific exercises and practice strategies. Training sessions with her were longer but they paid off; she became world No. 7 at one point.

Calculating: The last 'C' is somewhat of a combination of the previous gendered aspects of elite sports training—that girls are more prone to over analysis of their own gameplay and strategy, whereas boys tend to be foolhardy and more reckless.

Again, this goes back to the values that boys and girls have been socialized to embrace but both are actively harmful to an athlete's ability to play well. Overthinking tends to cause players to tense up, become worried, turn inward, become easily distracted and thrown off, while foolhardy players will forget strategy and deftness for brute strength and self-aggrandizement that is easily read and countered. Both are harmful and both require a re-centreing of what is most important and strong about an athlete's gameplay.

The way this kind of overthinking affects gameplay can be somewhat insidious. For example, I have seen dozens of female athletes lose rallies because they did not take the chance to hit the open space ending at the point when they had an opportunity. When we work together to review what happened, it is always a variation of the same story—they saw the chance they had but figured that the opponent also saw that opening and thus would be planning a counter plan to their plan since the move was obvious. If that were true, then the intelligent thing to do would be to develop a counter plan to the opponent's counter plan to their original plan, i.e., not going for the obvious and easily countered play and taking a riskier shot to continue the rally instead. This shot may seem to be the wrong move on the surface but would be the right move if the athlete was correct in thinking that her opponent knew that they knew that she was going to go for the easy shot and were planning accordingly.

And this was only one layer of overthought: What if her opponent planned for her planning ahead? Since not making the obvious move is itself somewhat of an obvious move, the best thing to do would be to take the open shot since her opponent would be thinking that she would be thinking that her opponent would be thinking that she would be thinking that it would be a wrong move...and thus it would end up being a good move? Deeper and more nonsensical inward thinking continues on and on like this when she could have just taken the shot and won.

To a degree, this kind of analysis can be very helpful in outwitting an opponent but when it becomes this convoluted and paralysing, as it tends to with girls who struggle with the aforementioned socialized self-consciousness, it is only a hindrance. The same is true with boys on the other end of things. Boys will usually screw up by not thinking ahead enough, making them predictable and thus easily manipulated.

Like I said, none of these are hard and fast rules, but it is important to understand the various gendered impulses that athletes may have and where they actually come from as this can only lead to a more holistic understanding of who your athlete is, both on and off the court. You should not rely on conventional wisdom and gendered assumptions. You need to do your research, put the work in to really connect with your players and understand the history and context of the world your players inhabit. In my experience, girls tend to take more nuance and patience to train but the reward is almost always higher; the extra time and care to personalize your approach really does pay off.

14

INDIVIDUALITY

If you would indulge me, I would like to take a moment to discuss just how influential Andre Agassi was not just in the world of tennis but also in how the rest of the world viewed tennis as a whole. He is, outside of the Williams sisters, the most well-known tennis player of all time. He was a pioneer of personal style and flair, even in ways that he does not get credit for. He popularized saying goodbye to the crowd at the end of a match well before it was a mainstream thing to do; he wore creative outfits on and off the court (who can forget his iconic denim shorts from 1988 US Open?); and he invented what is now referred to as the 'Agassi Knot', an anti-vibration measure for his racket that, because of our lack of foresight to establish a patent, is now a fundamental part of the tennis equipment sold by both big companies and small businesses such as little novelty silicon dampeners shaped like flags, emojis, superhero symbols, obscene gestures, flowers and brand logos, that sell for two to five dollars a pop.

Even before his fame, Agassi always stuck out—an entirely unique player in every facet of his life. If you have read his autobiography, the tremendous *Open: An Autobiography*, ghostwritten by J.R. Moehringer, you know how rigorous his early training schedule was as a child, and how, at 13, he moved from Nevada to Florida to attend our academy and avoided stagnation as he improved his game. You also know about his rebellious behaviour. Like I said in Chapter 2, it is hard to deny that Agassi hated tennis on a deep level given how he talks about both the sport and his father's abusive behaviour, but it is also hard to deny that, because of how hard he worked at it and how quickly it became his lifeblood, he was a genius at it. That kind of performance does not come without giving it your all, enthusiasm notwithstanding.

Once, when we were doing a drill involving cross-court forehands, Agassi instinctively hit the ball over to the other corner to finish the point. I tried to correct him, pointing out that the goal of the drill was to practise engaging in prolonged rallies, but Agassi argued back, saying the drill was unrealistic. If this were a real game, he would never keep the point going when he had the chance to end it. He was going to end it as soon as he could every time. Of course, wearing his opponents down by making them run back and forth to keep a rally going became a staple of his play style, but only when it gave him a tactical advantage. He never toyed with his opponent when he could just to win the point.

I mention all of this to point out that individuality is another huge component in developing elite athletic skills. As a coach or a parent, you should not only know that every player is distinct, with their strengths, weaknesses, styles, tendencies and patterns but also know what those components are for each athlete. Agassi, for example, was a very physical learner, unafraid to speak his mind; someone who relied on tactile work on the court rather than extensive theory or intellectual breakdown. This is not to say that he was not smart, just that his approach to training was his own. In Chapter 1, I talked about the role played by genetics in determining an athlete's skill level. This is by no means a hard and fast science but it is another unique component to an athlete that needs to be understood, especially with regards to their total development. At high performance institutions and Olympic training centres, they make every student take a variety of tests to measure various physical and cognitive components to establish a baseline and understand what unique point each child is starting from. This helps coaches handcraft programmes and drills to the needs of specific athletes. They test things like body type, physical skills, cognitive skills, behaviour capabilities, emotional intelligence and much more.

This is the sort of thing that is vital to understanding not just the athlete and how to better train them but also what kind of games or gameplay styles they can realistically expect to implement at the earliest stages in their development. Breaking down the potency and amount of slow-twitch muscle fibre to fast-twitch muscle fibre, for example, results in radically different sports getting chosen over others. Swimming and long-distance running are more gradual and thus benefit from more slow-twitch muscle fibre, whereas sports like tennis, martial arts and gymnastics are more suited for fast-twitch muscle fibres.

The heart of individuality is not just in specialized training but in a constant aura that exists both on and off the court. It is crucial that coaches and parents understand what makes their child special and lean into it in order for their child to thrive in whatever it is that they are doing. When we talk about a child becoming the next superstar in whatever sport they are investing, we are not talking about direct emulation of the superstar's style but rather being able to match their impact on their sport or industry. Nobody but Agassi can be Agassi, but someone could be as big as Agassi; and as children grow older and begin to try on different 'hats', both competitively and socially, you begin to see what traits make them who they are. I will cover this more in depth in another section of the book how these traits figure heavily into the marketing of athletes as well. These traits can help establish their brands—the rebelliousness of Agassi, the gentlemanliness of Nishikori, the sex appeal of Kournikova, the elegance and positive humility of Pierce, etc.

Honing and maintaining this kind of consistent persona can be difficult, especially when external forces, among them industry staples like rabid fans and constant media coverage—are testing you in a thousand ways. Martín 'El Loco' Palermo is a good example of keeping this kind of aura alive during hardship. Palermo is a former Argentinian soccer player who ended up becoming Boca Juniors' all-time top scorer with 236 goals. When we got the chance to interview him before he spoke to the students at my academy, we were impressed by how charismatic he was despite no longer playing and upholding his famous 'El Loco' image—a persona of intensity and unrelenting strength. Eventually, we asked him about the moment that, even more than his total number of goals with Boca, made him (in) famous. In 1999, during a game against Colombia, Palermo failed to score three penalty kicks in a row. The first two bounced squarely off the goal and the third was caught by the keeper. He was ridiculed by opponents and fans alike and even managed to get into the Guinness World Records for his impressive fumble.

While frustrated in the moment, he knew he had to remain composed, and for several games after that, he would be surrounded by the constant buzz of vehement harassment and personal insults by supposed fans. When we asked about how he managed to keep his cool, he responded that he felt that he was born to be an athlete, not just for the success of it but the total lifestyle of it and he accepted both the ups and the downs of it. His aura of confidence and determination didn't come from other people, not the fans, his coach or his family, but from within himself. He had a champion's mindset and was able to view the game beyond some unfortunate failures. In no time at all, fans were switching from hateful chants to screams of encouragement whenever he made a good play, sometimes even during the same game.

We can see subtle examples of this kind of individuality everywhere, even in the small things an athlete does. For example, in golf, watching Tiger Woods simply arrive at a tournament tells us a lot. He parks his car in the unloading area and does not speak to anyone. His head is down and he is quiet and focussed. Phil Mickelson, on the other hand, is a totally different story. He parks his car in plain view of everyone, smiling at people as he gets out, shaking hands and greeting the crowd with friendly waves as he makes his way to the clubhouse. Neither of these approaches are better than the other; each athlete is just doing what is most natural for them as individuals.

Another factor of individuality that is often overlooked and forgotten is that of approach. The most unique figures are visionaries. They see the world in different ways, see opportunities and patterns other people miss and think about and devise the best strategies not just to win but to totally change the game forever. This is not only true for any sport but also for any other field of passion or expertise. Think about people like Walt Disney or Steve Jobs; they may not have always been the ones doing the physical labour required to make their ideas work but they pioneered and revolutionized their industries all the same. Their ideas were unique, daring and went against conventional wisdom. They stuck to their guns and were able to become, among other things, the standard against which all other competitors were judged. In a similar vein, every student I have worked with who ended up becoming world No. 1 never liked being compared to anyone else. Even at a young age, they wanted to carve out their own place, one made especially for them and all the unique things they were doing.

It is that kind of thinking and commitment that needs to be encouraged and fostered in young athletes and that needs to be honed based on their strengths as an individual. A good coach does not get intimidated by the hard-headedness of these kinds of players; rather, a good coach directs and guides, with clear and pertinent information, a player to the heights they know the players can reach. Of course, this also has to be balanced with a certain kind of constant expectation. You do not want to stifle this kind of energy but you also do not want them to be able to do or say whatever they want, to become entitled and spoiled. You still, on the whole, know better than them, and finding a way to ground them without restricting them is tough and requires a lot of trial and error. This kind of player makes us step up, be our best selves and bring everything we have to the realization of their dreams. Coaching this kind of athlete is undoubtedly difficult but the most rewarding type of work that you will ever do.

When it comes to identifying what exactly makes a young athlete unique, there is a popular acronym that I use to help my staff and students remember the five components that both build and hamper individuality—OCEAN. It stands for **O**penness, **C**onscientiousness, **E**xtraversion, **A**greeableness, **N**euroticism.

The first three are positive traits. **Openness** is all about someone's enthusiasm for the unknown, for tackling and solving new problems and following their intense drive. They welcome new ideas related and unrelated to the sport and are open to different experiences in general.

Conscientiousness is a player's mindfulness when it comes to setting and following goals as well as adapting to changes in order to keep effective structure and time management. This applies to how they spend their time off the court, away from the sport—their hobbies, passions and interests.

Extraversion refers to not only an athlete's ability to withstand the pressures of being centre stage but also about their desire to be there, which is governed by their belief in themselves. This stems from emotional and perceptual intelligence and their ability to see and react to the world with them at the centre. Selfishness is a core part of the elite athlete's lifestyle, not only because what they do is inherently uncooperative but also because their career is focussed on them as an individual. An athlete needs to be extraverted enough to be the right kind of egotist; the kind that is able to take care of themselves and put themselves ahead of other people in a healthy and mandatory way.

The other two attributes of OCEAN are things that are negative; things that are unique to each player but ultimately stand anything down that is uniquely positive about them. **Agreeableness**, sort of the opposite of extraversion, is someone's tendency to put other people ahead of themselves and not think and see the world in terms of their goals as an athlete. Sure, having too grand of a self-image can make you a detached jerk but that is ultimately way less devastating for your career than having the opposite problem. This also refers to putting too much stock into what people think of you. Unless the feedback is directly helping your game, it does not really matter.

Neuroticism is the last component of OCEAN. This facet is all about mindset. People who are constantly negative, sad and defeatist, as well as people who overthink and get trapped in their own heads, do not do well in the world of elite sports. You need to be able to properly process these feelings, which are, to a certain extent, natural while not getting bogged down by them.

Like I said before, individuality is often an aura, a somewhat intangible weight that a player carries with them. Not only can you spot such players out of a crowd but you can see this aura strengthen and develop over time. A good coach can recognize what makes his players unique, but a great coach pulls these things out and turns them into an athlete's greatest strength, on and off the court, carving a legacy that lasts forever.

SECTION IV

THE MENTAL PART

15

IMAGINATION

At my academy, we ask all the players the same question when they first arrive—a question to spark within them the same baseline understanding of what they are here to do. We simply ask them 'What is your dream?' Not what their goal is or what they hope to accomplish at some point but what their dream is—what they want more than anything else and what keeps them motivated even through the most gruelling phases of stagnation and self-doubt.

Every champion that I have ever trained has had the same answer. They have looked me dead in the eye and replied 'I'm going to be No. 1 in the world.' There is no question in this statement, no doubt in its syntax or hesitation in its make-up. This answer is stated as a fact, a matter of time, a declaration of purpose and promise. We talked in the last chapter about champions having an aura and an unmistakable air about them. This is where it begins—the confidence and talent to begin making their dreams a reality by taking the first step: imagining, and thus knowing, that their most lofty and ultimate goal is not only possible but inevitable.

This principle of imagination is not, to be clear, the same thing as merely 'wanting it'. Every underdog sports movie wants you to believe that the key to wild success is your drive alone, which is patently and demonstratively false. The version of imagination that is crucial to an athlete's success is not simply about desire. It is about a shift in perception and a change in the way you see yourself and what is possible. Imagination is not so much about wanting anything as it is about knowing these things and their outcomes to be true before they happen. The kind of focus and dedication and single-minded energy it takes to become an elite athlete means that you have to make your dreams a reality before they can become real; you have to latch on to that in order to survive. We can think about John F. Kennedy's famous speech about going to the moon, about humanity's instinct to strive and push the boundaries of what is thought possible and the iconic phrase about doing things not because they are easy but because they are hard. When you think about what it takes to play elite sports, what it mentally, physically and emotionally takes to climb the ranks, imagination is this kind of determination—determination in the deepest and most holistic sense of the word.

Luckily, things like this are not an abstract concept for the young athletes that rely on this sense of potential for motivation. Technology has undoubtedly helped young athletes foster this kind of imagination. Since they can now review, analyse and soak up information about their heroes, their history, interviews and videos of their successes and failures at virtually every stage of their careers at an unprecedented rate. The internet has made their dreams more accurate, tactile and tangible. This leads them naturally to the concept of the 'invisible man' in training, where the players practise with a specific pro in mind and try to beat an imaginary adversary who they are always competing against. As coaches, we encourage this and lace our criticism with the specific names of these 'invisible men' as a constant reminder. Can you beat Novak Djokovic with that shot? Rafael Nadal would have reached that ball easily. Your service needs to improve to beat Serena Williams. You have to make contact with the ball earlier if you are going to outplay Roger Federer. Maria Sharapova, after losing 6–0 at the Junior Orange Bowl at 13, told me that she was not practising to beat just anyone but practising to beat Serena Williams. It was always on her mind—at every moment and in every aspect of her training—and five years later, she faced Williams in the Wimbeldon finals and, against all odds, beat her. Beyond the skill of her gameplay, she won because she had been training for this moment, playing this match over and over again for the past half-decade.

This also speaks to the temporal phenomenon that young athletes become privy to. Within the realm of elite athleticism, time shrinks and becomes attenuated in specific ways. In other disciplines, even competitive ones, the idea of potentially meeting and maybe even becoming more successful than your heroes is often a lofty fantasy. It can happen, but it is not very common and it means something different when we are talking about artistic fields or business numbers. Elite athletes, though, have to adjust to the fact that not only will they inevitably meet and play against their heroes but that it will happen soon, very soon, likely around the time they turn 18 if all goes well. Idealization works differently because imagination works differently. It is not about what could happen but about what is almost certainly going to happen and keeping up your end of the bargain. You spend years imagining yourself competing at the highest level of play against the best of the best, and then, suddenly, you blink and you are there.

In this way, the kind of imagination that I am talking about is a choice, something that athletes must actively and consciously use to keep themselves motivated. Jorge was no stranger to the challenge and the loneliness that often goes hand in hand with his passion. The schedule of a professional swimmer is exhausting; there are 2 training sessions every day, one before the sun comes up and one from late afternoon until the sun goes down. This happens, more often than not, in the cold and dark every day, rain or shine. Jorge would swim a lap, look at the big clock next to the pool, timing his break so that he was allowed a breather (that only lasts a few seconds), then he would do another lap. Over and over and over again. A professional swimmer usually swims around 14,000 m a day or 98,000 m a week. The kind of motivation needed to put in that much work consistently as well as all the other lifestyle choices, like a diet that has to be followed to make this schedule work, go beyond simple desire or dedication. It requires a clear visualization of what you are working towards, one so lucid that it becomes its own kind of reality. Jorge's team would have him conjure the scene of the Munich Games, focussing on every detail—the smell of the chlorine coming from the pool, his nerves as he was perched on top of the block, the sound of the starting gun and the roar of the crowd as he leapt into the water. They asked him to imagine what it would feel like to show up and represent his flag and his country, to see himself wearing the national uniform and to be surrounded by the best athletes in the world. This was the thing that made it possible for him to show up every day and put his all into every one of those 14,000 m.

Similarly, imagination is about understanding and striving toward the opportunities that one receives once they have reached their goals and achieved their dreams. For instance, a young child always dreamed of flying and of all the places that she would be able to go to if she would get the opportunity to travel. When she asked her parents how she would be able to fly in an airplane and see more of the world besides her old haunt in Amsterdam, they told her that she would have to become a world-class tennis player. This was the spark she needed; she held on to this image through all the highs and lows of her training. Every sacrifice, every stroke, every sprint, every bite of food, every hour spent training when she wanted to do anything else was in service to finally be able to fly. Nationals were coming around and even though no one expected anything from her, as she was a relatively unknown player, she poured every ounce of herself into her training, and, when the time came, she won the whole thing. She went on to represent her country internationally and has since then travelled half the world, attributing her success to the dedication brought on by her imagination.

This principle of imagination does not just apply to players though. The coaches have to also have a seemingly endless capacity for hope, a belief in their players and the imagination to visualize the success they can reach. When Andre Agassi was 16, training under me and Nick Bollettieri, he started to flounder. Nick wanted me to give up on him and to get off what he called 'The Agassi Bus'. He wanted me to focus on players who actually seemed to care, showed signs of improvement and were not nearly as insubordinate. But I stuck with Agassi, knowing his potential and the power of what he was capable of. I saw him winning grand slams and becoming world No. 1. Even when Agassi himself faltered and did not seem to be able to imagine much of anything beyond his current discontent, I never faltered. The more he pushed my buttons, the more I dedicated myself to him as my personal project. I refused to let such talent go to waste and put everything I had into making sure that did not happen. In the end, we managed to turn a corner as a team, and in 2009, Agassi went on to say this about our relationship: 'Gabe was a very special part of my formative years and I appreciate all of the attention he gave my game. He took the time to care in an environment that was competitive and fast-paced. It is fair to say he has not only added to my game but has truly added to my life.'[11]

I used the power of imagination to motivate other young players as well. Every day, before and after practice, we would imagine playing the big events. We would talk about what they would do, how they would act and the kind of things they would spend their inevitable wealth on. The point was to keep them laser-focussed on their dream and remind them that it was possible if they were willing to work. In order for a child to start fostering their imagination, like any other aspect of professional athleticism, they must start early. If you are a parent, when was the last time you asked your child what their dreams were? The last time you

---

[11]gabejaramillo.com, https://bit.ly/3HMNEpX. Accessed on 10 February 2023.

overtly encouraged them to fantasize about their wildest ambitions and focus on ways to reach those goals rather than focussing on results? Unfortunately, we do not do this kind of work enough and our children suffer from it. Of course, there must always be a balance since this kind of support can easily slide into the kind of overbearing pressure that we talked about in the last chapter, but if we allow our children to dream, they become more motivated and that motivation is more organic. If we treat them like pros, they act like pros, and having a robust imagination is part of that process.

Imagination is all about perseverance and perspective, the ability to envision the world of your dream so thoroughly that it pushes you to make it a reality. Just like how the line between egotism as total narcissism and egotism as self-preservation in elite sports comes down to how it affects and bolsters your gameplay, so is it with delusion and unwavering imagination. Often, the difference is in the results, in being able to follow through and make your dream happen, in what that perspective drives you to do and how you do it.

16

FEARLESS

'No fear' is my first commandment. It is the principle on which all other aspects of a champion's attitude are based and is the most fundamental to understand. It is, in many ways, the linchpin holding together all three spheres of the game; the thing that defines the different parts of an athlete's talent more than anything else.

I like to think about the relationship of physical and mental components of an athlete's gameplay in terms of the relationship between diet and exercise with regards to fitness. If you are trying to work on your health, diet is undeniably the more crucial of the two halves, but you are never going to achieve the kind of body transformation most people look for in their fitness goals without working out as well. The same is true for becoming an elite athlete. Obviously, being able to physically perform the necessary actions to play a sport at a high level is the most fundamental thing, but you cannot become a champion without proper mental strength and understanding, and indeed, that strength is what allows an athlete to reach the physical prerequisites. 'No fear' is the foundational cornerstone of everything; it is the simplest but also the hardest to overcome

When my brother and I were kids, my mother would

often tell us stories with these sorts of principles at their core. This was partly because of how integral sports were for both of us growing up but also because my mother, similar to Andre Agassi during his Hall of Fame induction speech, understood that so many of the principles that define the best athletes and the best aspects of the games they play directly resonate with life itself. I remember the most vivid tale she spun, that of a shipwreck. The looming threat of trouble was signalled by dark clouds and brisk winds. A violent and unholy storm tore through the boat. Many people panicked, froze and drowned, leaving only a few proactive survivors on a meager life raft. The ensuing delirium during the search for land or help, the mental breakdowns and deaths of all but one survivor, the person strong enough to push through every obstacle and stay alive long enough to see rescue. These stories were often so lucid that they disturbed my brother and I but they always taught us a valuable lesson—succumbing to fear and panic only leads to further distress and dire consequences.

There are many ways to analyse and break down fear but understanding the scientific phenomenon behind the 'fight or flight' response is a helpful place to start. Mammals, when faced with a life-threatening situation, have a split-second involuntary physiological response—hormones change, adrenaline is released, muscles tense, the heartbeat quickens and beads of sweat begin to form all over their bodies. This is the body preparing itself to act in one of two ways—staying put and defending itself or fleeing the situation to safety as quickly as possible. It is important to note that this response is strictly biological and thus has no way of confirming the actual lethality of whatever is going on. This physical shift often occurs during perceived dangers, even if the perception of threat is subconscious. Stress and worry often cause this reaction, and this constant hormonal shift, when activated dozens and hundreds of times in unnecessary circumstances, can cause lasting damage.

This is the physical side of things, but the most potent aspect of fear, within not only our lives but also in sports, is the lasting doubt that it causes, which often ruins opportunities that otherwise would not have been a problem. Fear is a hang-up about what is to come in the future, an emotion that anchors you to the present moment while simultaneously demanding your attention in all kinds of places, displacing your focus in a way that keeps you from embodying your true potential. At its core, the idea of 'no fear' is all about betting on the future, on a belief in yourself and your abilities that goes beyond innate concerns. It is impossible for anyone to completely quell their fears, to negate their biological responses and to never feel worried or concerned but that does not mean you have to be controlled by these inevitabilities. To act without fear is not to dismiss its presence or impact but rather to work your way around it in a way that allows you to keep playing as well as you can.

At the end of the day, when you boil down all the matches, tactics and fancy philosophy, when an athlete is on the court in the heat of competition, they have two options—either they take the shot or they do not. Thus, the fact of the matter is that nothing gets done without risk, i.e., action in the face of the knowledge that you could fail and that your failure could have major consequences but that the potential reward is worth that chance. We can think about this in our own lives, how we need to get out of our comfort zones if we want to grow; in history, how figures like Nelson Mandela, Winston Churchill and Ida B. Wells accomplished all they did under the cloud of extreme risk; and how the top athletes often develop and pioneer the most cutting edge, and thus controversial, play styles and tactics.

Within the realm of sports, I'm a big proponent of the phrase 'calculated risk' because it encapsulates everything that living by no fear means. Again, the goal is not to eliminate all fear forever but rather to be able to control every facet of a situation that you have the power to in order not to submit to the poor judgment and bad plays that fear encourages. Knowing when and how to take risks is a big part of this mental component of the game. If an athlete just does any random play, hoping that it pays off, they are taking a risk but not one that is likely to pan out for them. In a way, any action a player does or does not take that could potentially backfire is a risk; it is just a matter of what the odds are and thus how severe the consequences of failure are. Like any other skill or muscle, learning to be more comfortable with risks is something that you grow and develop over time. This is why good coaches often encourage silly games, like the airport coin toss that I mentioned back in the chapter about competition. Getting an athlete, especially a young player early in their career, comfortable with taking chances in a low-stakes environment helps prime them for this kind of decision-making on the court. It also helps develop their eye for calculating risk; the player gets better at recognizing what they should do in any given circumstance because they have become used to being in situations where they have to assess these odds, even if it is on a more minor scale. Having a good understanding of strategy and tactical thinking is vital to overcoming and controlling fear.

One way that this manifests itself is in the application of aggressive play versus defensive play. Being on the defensive means that you are at the mercy of whatever your opponent decides to do. The fact that whatever counter-play you can come up with must directly respond to their actions means that they are in a position that allows them to take more risks while also having a sort of safety net to fall back on in the form of control over your immediate response. This is why so many of the best players in any sport are aggressive without being stupid about it and why players like Andre Agassi prefer to start a point aggressively. This aggression allows them to set the pace of the game and get valuable information on how their opponent is going to respond. This is a similar principle as to why boxers throw short jabs at one another during the beginning of a bout, jabs that are never meant to connect but meant to tell the player how their opponent flinches, giving them information to figure into the calculation of future blows. Learning to control fear is also about not giving any leverage to your opponent in these kinds of situations, too.

It is going to take years and years for a player to ever learn this 'no fear' principle, since this, like so many other things in elite sports, is not the kind of thing that you ever stop learning. Parents need to learn what their role is in supporting their children and encouraging them to take risks while also being smart. It is a fine line to walk, one that is unique to every athlete but there are some fundamental components that never change—failure should always be something to learn from, risk is a direct key to innovation, which is a direct key to constant improvement, fear is the best friend of stagnation, etc.

Another factor to consider while instiling this principle in your children is that they are, indeed, children, at least when they are starting out. Their naiveté is, at once, something that opens them up to experimentation while also something that makes them more likely to get burned and internalize that failure. Learning to cope with fear, to control and even direct it, is something that comes with time and maturity, and so, it should be worked on gradually. Understanding how children in general and your child specifically deal with both success and failure can give you insight on how to move forward in a productive way—on what things spark fear and what things put it to rest. For example, parents often want to bolster their child's confidence by hyping them up and telling them how well they are doing. In moderation, it can be encouraging but can also lead to expectational paralysis in the child. They want to impress and live up to the version of them you seem to have and they will burn themselves out and beat themselves up to try and get there, if their fear allows them to move at all in the first place.

I often use the analogy of mountain climbing when discussing this with my students. Another way to work on reducing your fear is to segment various challenges and break things down into more manageable chunks. If you set out to climb a mountain, never resting or stopping to adjust your course or to re-evaluate the state of your mission, then you are never going to reach the peak, and that is if you even manage to push past your fear of how overwhelming the task is to begin in the first place. If you look at professional mountain climbers, you will see that they have an entirely different system. They map out multiple paths in advance, rest frequently at elaborate camps along the way, reroute their course if something unforeseen happens and come prepared in advance for mistakes and miscalculations. All of this, along with persistent, grinding patience, allows them to overcome their obstacles and reach the top. And the cliché is as true for tennis as it is for anything else—the view at the top is made all the more satisfying by the journey to it.

Another analogy that I use with my students is that of taming a horse. Fear is, in many ways, naturally stronger than us. We have to work hard to conquer it and keep it under control. We cannot worry about how we look while we are doing it, about whether or not we look elegant and collected in the face of terror. Focussing on that, rather than the actual breaking of the horse, is a surefire way to let fear overpower us.

This is why it is also so important, especially in the early stages of an athlete's career, to focus on development rather than results. Parents who expect their child to win every match and sweep every event are not only in for a rude awakening but are also actively harming their child's mental development with regards to the game by creating an environment choked by the fear of failure. No parent wants to harm their children, but unfortunately, when they do not control their emotions and make comments without thinking, they cause irreparable consequences. For example, comparing their child to other players (how can you lose to that boy you used to beat easily, that kid that does not practice, etc.). Losses and mistakes are key to the learning process and if a player is too afraid of messing up to try

something new, or indeed anything at all, their dreams are
as good as dead. There are more important things than
rankings and good win/loss ratio. These things come with
genuine development, if you put the time in to make that
happen.

Becoming fearless is one of the major principles of a
strong mental game. On the other side of fear is freedom,
which is an improvement that gives us great opportunities
to develop that immense talent. Courage is the fundamental
cornerstone that never ceases to grow and fear is the wall
that always needs to be broken down.

17

ATTITUDE

The third component to a strong mental game is a player's attitude. If 'no fear' is the most important component of an athlete's success then a resilient attitude is, in many ways, the most foundational element of continued success in the world of elite sports, in so much that it is key not only to an athlete's internal success but to their exterior image as well.

Having a good attitude in this industry goes beyond clichés about 'positive thinking'; it is about having a mindset that encourages self-reflection, growth and change as well as a perfect balance of arrogance and humility to continuously improve in a way that goes above and beyond rankings and stats. A good attitude is also vital for your overall physical health as a negative and pessimistic outlook can lead to anxiety and stress, which can lead to a variety of physical ailments like sluggishness, headaches, exhaustion, stomach trouble and insomnia, in addition to the mental weight it can put on you that affects your ability to perform as well as you can.

Contrary to popular belief, attitude is not something that you are stuck with naturally or something that you are unable to change. Of course, different people are going to be more prone to different modes of thinking on the scales of optimism/pessimism, realism/idealization and empathy/logic, etc., but these inclinations are not hard and fast. In a sense, fostering a positive attitude is a lot like learning a new skill. There are the foundational elements you need to get down in order to execute it on a basic level but then there are so many nuances about how we learn, how we change, how we adapt and get better at said skill in different situations over time.

There are four major components to one's attitude. They are as follows:

1. **Behaviour**: This refers to how someone reacts to external stimuli. This is not based so much on things like thought or emotion but rather on the environment one finds themselves in and how one chooses to respond to it.

2. **Character**: This refers to a person's core values and beliefs, who they are inside, the most honest and true version of themselves.

3. **Personality**: This refers to the way a person presents themselves to the world at large and how much what they show reflects their character. This is formed by the environment and various kinds of social pressure as well as internal integrity and morals, to a more or less equal degree.

4. **Temperament**: This refers to one's innate traits, levels of energy and enthusiasm, demeanour and their instinct to take risks. These things can shift and be adjusted depending on the situation, but are, for the most part, hardwired in a person as defaults that they will always fall back on.

So, let's break it down in this way. Imagine a nuclear submarine. **Behaviour** is how the submarine reacts to external elements, like the heat of the Caribbean Sea or the icy polar waters. **Character** is the entire internal computer system guiding the vessel. **Personality** is the outer body of the ship or the image it projects. Finally, **temperament** is how the submarine handles its environment, either smooth or rough, and this is the only part that is hard to change.

These facets of someone's attitude are constantly being molded and changed by many internal and external factors. They are always playing off one another in virtually limitless nuanced ways. Generally speaking, there are different ways for someone to 'train' their attitude within themselves.

They learn and change via observation and imitation from esteemed peers and personal heroes whom they admire. Or via the ingrained written and unwritten rules of high-performance athleticism. Or through principles that often have to do with giving yourself to something without complaint because you understand its importance such as 'always do what it takes, no matter what' or 'give one hundred percent in everything you do', etc.

Another way to train one's attitude is through acknowledging feedback—learning and changing via the genuine willingness to take complaints from coaches, parents, mentors and trainers when you are not responding to the training in the way that you should. A winning attitude leaves no room for ambiguity or negativity. Young athletes must know that they are responsible for their success or failure. Therefore, there are no excuses or explanations.

Another reason why a player's attitude is so important is that attitude is, essentially, a personal ideology, a set of values and principles that govern not only how you act and respond to the (let's not forget) incredibly harsh and unforgiving world of professional athleticism but also how you act and respond to everything in that world and your place in it. Your attitude directly affects every aspect of your life, both on and off the court. It affects your training and its effectiveness, your marketability and brand consistency, your ability to learn from failure, your knowledge acquisition skills as well as how effective you are at communicating, etc. Attitude ties together every other component of elite training and boils it down to one underlying interaction. Attitude is a combination of the mental and the physical, the emotional and the logical, the interior and the exterior. Attitude is also constantly shifting with time, growth and experience. All the best pro athletes have fostered great attitudes because, regardless of any individual grace, niceness or positivity, they have had to. You simply cannot survive the myriad obstacles this world throws at you without a great attitude.

Diego Maradona is considered to be one of the greatest soccer players of all time. His career was too long and decorated to outline here in full but his success as both a player and a coach, outside of his immense amount of skill, can be attributed largely to his attitude and how committed he was to constant improvement. When he was transferred to Napoli, a notoriously bad team among the Italian league, he was worshiped as a saviour, to the point where one local newspaper wrote that even though Naples lacked a 'mayor, houses, schools, buses, employment and sanitation, none of this matters because we have Maradona'.[12] And they were right. He was able to encourage his teammates and lead them to multiple championship victories.

This is not to say that Maradona is a perfect person or an unwavering saint. Around this time, he also was also pretty severely addicted to drugs, racking up fines for missing practices, meetings and getting caught up in a handful of personal scandals. A lot of this kind of behaviour ended up affecting his health years later as he dealt with a slew of personal problems. When he moved to Mexico and began working as a coach (an impressive feat in its own right, since most people only have a knack for one role or the other), he could barely walk and was in a lot of physical pain. Despite this, his attitude—his ability to rally those around him and to inspire greatness— never faltered and was, in fact, more inspiring given all his ailments. That is the point of having a strong and irresistible attitude. It is not that it makes you invincible or immune to controversy or hardship but that it allows you to never waver, to be honest with yourself and to be consistent. Having a champion's attitude keeps the best players anchored in the midst of the endless chaos that makes up the world of elite sports.

Andre Agassi is, once again, a great example of someone who did not let their unfortunate circumstances affect their attitude or corrode their personal ideology. After his divorce from Brooke Shields, his ranking plummeted. Rather than

[12]Millar, Colin, 'Barcelona Boss Xavi Points Out Mistake With Diego Maradona Statue in Naples', *Irish Mirror*, 24 February 2022, https://bit. ly/3IaXT8O. Accessed on 10 February 2023.

cashing in on his fame, using his previous world No. 1 ranking to score wild cards and buys for events in order to expedite his journey back to the top, he decided to stick to his principles and reach the dizzying heights that he had been on before by starting from the bottom. He had to make his own calls, retrieve his own balls, keep his own score and wade through his humiliation while being mocked by other players. But this is the kind of commitment to a personal brand and an attitude that has made Agassi a player with such a robust legacy. He stuck to his principles and did not take the easy way out for convenience's sake.

To this point, parents tend to try and shelter their children and try to do that protective work for them. As a person with children of their own, I definitely understand that urge but it is one that has to be resisted. The only avenue a person has to develop a proper and healthy attitude and the only avenue they have to a holistic mental and emotional state, is growth from experience, both positive and negative. Rather than trying to bolster the child by hyping up every victory and quickly ignoring every loss in order to keep them happy and feeling good about themselves and their potential, or giving them easy outs to every bit of hardship, you do them a greater service by allowing them to tackle these things themselves by being there to support and guide them, but ultimately, allowing them to grow into their own emotional ideology in response to their time in this occupation. You have to be honest with them and with yourself. If this means quitting, finding a different sport or passion altogether then that is what it means. This is, ultimately, the difference between those who are champions and those who are not—the ones who were meant to thrive in this field remain, meet every challenge, overcome every stumble and are strengthened by this exposure.

Parents and coaches have to think along these lines as well, although the stakes of your actions have, in many ways, a much greater impact on the young athletes, since you are the one guiding them virtually every minute of every day in the thing that they are devoting their lives to. You have to think about small things—how you conduct yourself and how you ask your children–athletes to conduct themselves in order to build their attitude bit by bit. I, for one, never sit down. I am with them the whole time, standing up straight, giving off an aura of confidence, control and authority that is not dictatorial. I do everything I can to be an example for these young athletes.

Maintaining a high-performance attitude is a choice that must be trained and reinforced from an early age. Parents and coaches play a critical role in helping young people develop a healthy mindset. Based on proper routines that can be engraved day after day, practice after practice until it becomes their automatic response. These athletes learn from all experiences, positive and negative. Jorge, getting ready for the Olympic games, used to remind himself that swimming was challenging. The only way to achieve excellence was by mastering every take-off, turn, stroke and sprint. He demanded the same execution level from himself every day, not just every 4 years. That is the attitude of a champion. Everybody that met Jorge immediately recognized his arrogance, high goals, exuberant confidence and toughness. He embodies the very temperament of an Olympian.

Developing a great attitude is not something that

happens overnight. This can seem like a curse, especially when the athlete is dealing with bouts of precociousness, angst or uncertainty. But what this time also means is that one's attitude can always mature and change for the better. You can learn from everyone in your life and from every experience that you have had to strengthen your mental fortitude and become the best athlete you possibly can be.

18

ROUTINES

Once, a group of war veterans started working as bodyguards for an international company. They were dedicated to patrolling, escorting and protecting high-ranking officials from harm. They still had to prepare, with the highest regard to discipline, for weapons training and hand-to-hand combat. The armoured car drivers carried out training, refining manoeuvres; radio operators were always attentive and studying. The intelligence part was the most important and they used to say that it was already late when one had to resort to weapons.

Every day, the bodyguards arrived an hour before the work started. They used that time to enlist their equipment and clean it carefully; they thoroughly carried out every detail and the drivers and radio operators did the same. All this was more than a routine; it was total perfection; 15 minutes before starting the mission, they checked each other's equipment to ensure that everything was in perfect order. Colonel Vallejo used to tell his men, 'We are what we repeatedly do, routines have to become habits, these daily preparations have to be executed with intention and purpose, with no alternatives. Enforcing these routines, our chances of survival increase or diminish.'[13] This degree of discipline and respect for purposeful routines, always in search of perfection, stuck in my mind and are values that I have inculcated in our athletes today. Routine, as a component of an athlete's life, goes well beyond schedules and set drills. It is a fundamental part of building an athlete's mental stability and establishing a thorough and proper work ethic. In many ways, routine is to repetition what content is to form. Routine is the content, i.e., what you are actually going to do over and over again. It encompasses a wide range of actions, both pre- and post-practice. Repetition, on the other hand, is the form that that content takes.

Many people ask me what all champions have in common and I answer that one of the main characteristics that they all demonstrate from an early age is discipline and consistency with routines. Everyone arrives half an hour before training starts, gets all their equipment ready and warms up to avoid wasting time. Once the practice is over, they have a cool-down routine. They keep perfecting themselves in their professional careers. These habits give them a sense of serenity.

For example, tennis players, in particular, have the capacity to make the courts a real mess. Beyond their rackets, players bring all kinds of things to practice—four or five cans of new tennis balls, several towels, untold amounts of plastic water bottles, energy bars, turn grips, Band-Aids, etc. They usually leave everything lying around

---

[13]This information is based on the author's personal experiences and interactions.

at the end of their practices or warm-ups. While some might not be as bothered by this as long as they can still play effectively, Agassi would never stand for his court to be less than spotless. He would spend the first few minutes of every practice making everything immaculate before he even thought about hitting a ball. It became a part of his routine. The clean court gave him a feeling of organization and calmness.

Routine is often about manifesting a sense of mental preparedness that gives the athlete a clear mindset and an advantage in their strategy. Once, a few years ago, I went to an event in Mexico City. I was travelling with two prominent young players. The events committee wanted their best juniors to compete in conjunction with my players, and when their students arrived on the court, you could immediately tell that they were not as well-prepared. They came on only carrying a few rackets and a towel and it was clear by their movements and general energy level that they had not warmed up. I saw this as an opportunity not to shame these children but to explain to them and the gathered crowd how thoroughly prepared my students, four years their junior, were in comparison. The audience chose a player and he explained the warm-up technique and showed the contents of his tennis bag, packed and prepared identically to how a professional would do it.

As he explained what was in the bag, he made sure to dive into nuances that most people would not even consider. For instance, he had five different rackets, all with their own unique tensions to not only give him comfortable backups in case the strings on one of them broke but to be able to adapt appropriately to the unfamiliar altitudes of Mexico

City. He had also brought along two pairs of shoes, one for hard court and one for clay, since, when he had visited the club the night before to ask questions about the matches the following day, he had been told that the type of surface he was to play on would depend on the weather. This is an example of the preparation of a highly competitive athlete.

Most elite players have a strict set of routines that they alone are responsible for from an early age. They arrive at training with time to prepare everything they need—new tape for fingers, changing racket grips, freshly laced shoes, a thermos of water filled with electrolytes and snacks to eat during breaks. They also warm-up to be physically and mentally prepared for their workout. Finally, they cool down with either gentle running or cycling, stretching to prevent injury at the end of the day. This is in addition to monitoring their diet and analysis of their game and the professionals they admire. Every athlete who takes the sport seriously prides themselves on having a proactive and consistent routine in all facets of the game (habits before, during and after training). And this is for a straightforward reason—you cannot become an elite athlete if you do not adhere to a structured and planned routine.

Another kind of routine that can give athletes a sense of calmness are rituals, little motions or actions that can help create a feeling of stability. They are anchors that force them to slow down and do not allow them to speed up, especially in times of more pressure. Maria Sharapova developed a celebratory ritual early on that she used until she retired. After winning a point, she used to put the racquet in her non-dominant hand, smiling or nodding, performing some kind of a positive response, closing her right fast and yelling,

'Come on!', before turning and walking to the baseline. Her breathing control was next, to help with her relaxation. She took time to make a tactical plan for the next point at the baseline. Her back was to her opponent. After she regrouped, Maria moved back to serve or return, moving her feet to get her heart rate up. She played at a fast pace and the entire process between points lasted only 15 seconds. This type of ritual can be observed in a soccer player before they execute a penalty kick or in a basketball player before they take a free throw.

People have noticed that Nadal has a lot of rituals that he performs and he has spoken on them, saying things like: 'I put the two bottles down at my feet, in front of my chair to my left, one neatly behind the other, diagonally aimed at the court. Some call it superstition, but it's not. If it were superstition, why would I keep doing the same thing over and over whether I win or lose? It's a way of placing myself in a match, ordering my surroundings to match the order I seek in my head,'[14] and 'The last part of the ritual, as important as all the preparations that went before, was to look up, scan the perimeter of the stadium, and search for my family members among the blur of the Centre Court crowd, locking their exact coordinates inside my head. [...] I don't let them intrude on my thoughts during a match—I don't ever let myself smile during a match—but knowing they are there, as they always have been, gives me the peace of mind on which my success as a player rests. I build a

---

[14]Chase, Chris, 'The Definitive Guide to Rafael Nadal's 19 Bizarre Tennis Rituals', *USA Today: For the Win*, 5 June 2014, https://bit.ly/3JTLMyr. Accessed on 9 February 2023.

wall around myself when I play, but my family is the cement that holds the wall together.'[15]

It is up to a coach to be able to identify what kind of actions an athlete becomes taken with and why they feel like they must perform them. This is another aspect of **individuality** that we talked about in the last chapter and another thing that a coach has to be cognizant of as their relationship with their athlete develops, even if the athlete prefers to keep them private. Jimmy Arias, for instance, only confirmed my suspicion that one of his tennis rituals was always to serve the first ball during the warm-up before a real match until well after he retired.

This is the point where I should point out that routines and rituals should always be either a productive and proactive move, or a lateral and harmless idiosyncrasy. When rituals get out of hand, they can become superstitions habits that a player relies on for success even though they have nothing at all to do with their actual skill set. We can see many different examples of this, even in the best and most famous athletes—Björn Borg used to always wear his FILA shirt and not shave until the tournament was over; Michael Jordan used to wear his University of North Carolina shorts under his uniform when he was with the Bulls; Serena Williams brings her shower sandals to the court as a good luck charm and Cristiano Rolando has to be the first one off the plane but the last to get off the bus.

The examples are endless. This kind of behaviour is not the worst thing for an athlete and can even be helpful

---

[15]Nadal, Rafael and John Carlin, *Rafa: My Story*, Little Brown Book Group, 2011.

if it gives the athlete a sense of calm before the storm of competition but it can become an issue when they start to rely on this more than real training and the actual skill they possess. Superstitions can become detrimental to their game if they are not contained within a reasonable context and it is often up to the coach to toe the line between encouraging what makes the players unique and helps them feel like they can play better and not allowing these small superstitions to ruin their mental game. Simply put, a routine is a strict habit, often micromanaged, that gives the athlete a sense of serenity. A ritual is a small action that helps ground the athlete by keeping him anchored so he does not rush. A superstition is an illusion that an athlete has placed too much emphasis on, to the point that it hampers his ability to compete.

All of this, especially the spectrum of routine and superstition, is a balancing act that is hard to accomplish; one that, depending on what kind of athletes you are training, you have to learn the hard way to really be able to implement properly. My first major experience with superstitions was during the Italian Open. I was travelling with two outstanding athletes who were, at the time, both in the top 10 in the world. They both had very solitary routines that they wanted me to take part in and so I found myself pulled in two different directions. I had to have breakfast, lunch and dinner with each of them separately, sitting at the same table every day and eating the same thing. They expected me to be there for every aspect of their routine, before, during and after their matches. So when rain fell and their events got double-booked for the same time, they both expected me to be at their competitions, not the other's. It was an impossible double bind. I did what was best under the circumstances—watching both of their semi-finals on TV back at the tournament restaurant. Still, my failure to adhere to their strict superstitions threw something off. They both lost their matches, Carling Bassett-Seguso to Chris Evert and Lisa Bonder to Martina Navratilova. Our rapport was compromised, our relationship never recovered and I ended up losing both of them as students.

Parents and coaches, you, of course, want to support what makes kids unique. You want to encourage proper routines and honour rituals that help keep them grounded during the stress of competition. All of this is to strengthen their mental game but you must be careful not to let these things get out of hand. My situation was inevitable in many ways but such strong reliance on the tricks of superstition was not. So, stick to the part of the process that makes sense, can bring calm to the athlete and stay away from the ephemeral.

SECTION V

A PLAYER'S SUPPORT SYSTEM

19

PARENTS

In many ways, this is the chapter of the book that is central to what I am trying to do here. I wrote this book to provide guidance for parents who are raising elite athletes and while everything that I have talked about up until this point is also crucial in developing various facets of success, a lot of elite athleticism is about relationships, and none is as impactful, especially in the earliest years of a child's career, than the athlete's relationship with their parents.

Firstly, while it might seem obvious, I think it is important to establish that a lot of research has been conducted on the correlation between a child's parental dynamic and their success in their sport. Thomas G. Power and Christi Woogler, in their 1994 paper, 'Parenting Practices and Age-Group Swimming: A Correlational Study', found that '...parental support was positively associated with child enthusiasm, whereas parental performance outcome goals and directiveness showed curvilinear effects',[16] meaning that children were able

---

[16]Power, Thomas G. and Christi Woogler, 'Parenting Practices and Age-Group Swimming: A Correlational Study', *Research Quarterly for Exercise and Sport* Vol. 65, No. 1, pp. 59–66, April 1994, https://bit.ly/3YmBdYV. Accessed on 10 February 2023.

to get really immersed in their game when parents only had a moderate amount of direct involvement in their training. In 1993, Robert Brustad published an article titled 'Who Will Go Out and Play? Parental and Psychological Influences on Children's Attraction to Physical Activity'[17] that found a similar positive relationship between parental encouragement and a child's own perceived competence. In their book, *Talented Teens: The Roots of Success and Failure*, researchers Mihaly Csikszentmihalyi, Kevin Rathunde Samuel Whalen and Maria Wong found that healthy and robust dynamics between parents and their children fosters growth, saying, 'In general, healthy development is increasingly seen as happening in a context where both autonomy and attachment and connection with parents are highly valued.'[18] This applies outside of the world of tennis or even sports specifically. K.D. Sloane's research on parental daily involvement in childhood passions, things ranging from art to writing to music to dance, positively contributed to their overall success, since their presence '…ensured the amount of practice time and prevented the child from practising mistakes or "playing around" instead of concentrating on the task […] the parents' involvement also served as motivation and

[17]Brustad, Robert, 'Who Will Go Out and Play? Parental and Psychological Influences on Children's Attraction to Physical Activity', *Pediatric Exercise Science*, Vol. 5, No. 3, pp. 210–23, 1993, https://bit.ly/3jMYhRD. Accessed on 10 February 2023.

[18]Csikszentmihalyi, Mihaly, Kevin Rathunde, Samuel Whalen and Maria Wong, *Talented Teenagers: The Roots of Success and Failure*, Cambridge University Press, 1996.

encouragement for the child's efforts'.[19]

I bring all this up to say that the facts are obvious—just like how you cannot foster an elite level of talent unless you start training as early as possible, a child cannot become their best, most talented self without the constant healthy support of their parents.

There is a relatively short window of time in a child's development in which their parents are most involved in their life and in their passions. It is a seven-year time-span, from ages six to 13, and you need to be ready to put your all into these years. During this phase, parents need to keep the following things in mind:

Parents must be realistic with their child: Not every child who starts down the path of their passion is going to wind up turning into a pro or make a living off of what they like to do. Regardless, the endeavour itself is often life-changing and should not be taken lightly. The kind of life lessons and principles that are instilled in people from their stints in sports or the arts are, with the proper kind of support and encouragement, overwhelmingly positive. While there is no excuse to approach anything your child wants to do or has the talent for with any kind of half measure, it is also wise to understand that not everyone is going to become the next transcendent master in everything they try their hand at. This should not be used to help enable your child to not try; however, if years of practice and training prove to be ineffective, it is important for them to know they are

---

[19]Sloane, K.D., 'Home Support for Successful Learning' *Advances in Reading/Language Research: A Research Annual Vol. 5.*, S.B. Silvern (ed.), JAI Press, 1991.

not a failure for reaching and realizing their limits or for taking what they have learnt from the time entrenched in this practice and applying it somewhere else.

One of my earlier students, Lihini Weerasuriya from Sri Lanka, was an absolute gem. She was the best tennis player in her country and had one of the deepest and most profound work ethic of anyone that I have ever met. Her whole family moved with her to the US in order to help her achieve her dream. Her hard-working attitude and sheer volume of practice were world-class but she could not translate that unstoppable drive into tournament results. Even as it became clear that there were many more girls her age with more talent and more potential, Lihini never gave up. She continued to practise, work and strive until the gap in skill and results became too stark to overcome. Lihini is now a well-known gynaecologist, one of the best in her field. She is not a failure and she and her family do not see her as one. She was able to take her work ethic, honed by years of athletic training, and apply it to something she really did have the talent for. This kind of healthy revelation and result are only possible when parents are honest with their kids in their encouragement and when their perception of their passion's role in their life is not two-dimensional or merely about winning.

Parents must be realistic with themselves: The only way that you are going to be able to embody the kind of support that your child needs to navigate their passion with all the verve of a champion is if you first know yourself and your parenting style in and out. In his book, *The Only Way to Win: How Building Character Drives Higher Achievement* *and Greater Fulfillment in Business and Life*, Jim Loehr outlines 4 different types of parents and how they tend to interact with their children. The first type are **the protectors**—the parents who intervene during all conflicts and make excuses for everything, never allowing their child to grow and develop their own autonomy and coping skills, preferring to smother and coddle them. The second type are **the pretenders**—the aloof parents who give the impression that they do not care about results when they secretly do; the ones who do not want to seem too involved and end up switching to the opposite extreme of cold distance. The third type are **the firesticks**—the intense and abusive hard-asses who only care about results; the parents who are constantly pushing their children with no thought to their overall well-being; who lord their power dynamic over their children with authoritarian consistency. The last type of parent is the most well-rounded and healthy, that of **the challenger**. This is the parent who is constantly working with their child in a respectful way to challenge them to do better and to grow. Their focus is often on larger, more holistic notions of development rather than individual wins or achievements.

While we all strive to be **challengers**, we all have our own tendencies and default actions that we tend to fall back on for a variety of reasons. To work with our children in the most effective way, we must recognize these tendencies in ourselves and develop strategies to understand why we are prone to certain behaviours and change them accordingly.

Take steps to optimize the ideology of yourself: Again, because the support of parents in the life of their child's passion is so vital, you have to make sure that you are operating in as healthy a way as you can on an ideological level, having a deep familiarity and understanding of the process. You have to know that you are not the coach and that your role is more fundamental—you are the general manager of the project while the coach is part of your team and works for you.

Since parents have an affective bond with their child, it is more advisable that they demand more from the coach and, in turn, the coach can put more pressure on the student, preserving the relationship between parents and children. Although it is difficult, you must be prudent in controlling your emotions. Do not do or say anything you might regret later. Stay classy because you have to be a role model as a team leader.

You also need to embrace the concept of 'no fear' that we talked about in the previous section. Part of being a leader is having the courage and, therefore, being able to instil that courage in the other members of your team. In addition, parents should encourage their children to make intelligent decisions and know that it is okay to make mistakes.

Take steps to optimize the ideology of the athlete: Likewise, it is vital to understand the ins and outs of each component that goes into the making of a good, mentally balanced athlete. For example, timing is crucial because motivation is an internal driver, as I said earlier. It can only come from within the athlete and has to be fostered and harnessed as earnestly as possible, as early as possible. The young athlete must feel supported and encouraged to move forward through developmental goals and not results.

It is essential to establish punctuality, preparation and routines early on. Making these core values work in all facets of their athletic career is, after all, the player's sole responsibility. The parent and their team must constantly motivate and encourage the principles behind the concrete actions and not just the actions themselves—things like effort, fighting spirit, perseverance, individuality, tolerance, courage and ambition.

Take steps to optimize the ideology of the parent–child relationship: It is not enough that you and your child understand each other. You must also understand the nuances of working together and ways to leverage them. Establish so-called 'pillar values' and never let these be questioned—honesty, discipline, attitude and respect. Set clear rules of engagement and conversation early on, including empathy and logical reasoning, to help manage insubordination when the child is older. There will surely come a time when your child will have complaints or will disobey you, so anticipate this and set rules on how to handle those disputes.

All parents should strive to know their children deeply and, at the same time, fully respect them with all their complexities without assuming that we know them better than anyone else. Finally, and most importantly, show them that a parent's love is unconditional.

Don't assume parents know nothing: This last one applies mainly to coaches but is important for parents as well. While the bulk of the actual training should, of course, come from the professionals, no one should assume that parents, even parents without a background in the passion being worked on, have nothing to offer their children beyond moral support. Famously, Andre Agassi's father, Emmanuel 'Mike' Agassi, was a boxer and it was his strategy of punches and counterpunches that led to the development of the power base-liner style of play, based on taking time away from the opponent by hitting early, that made Agassi successful.

Jimmy Arias's father, Antonio Arias, is another great example. He was an electrical engineer and a mathematics professor at the State University of New York at Buffalo (SUNY Buffalo) in New York. He became obsessed with the advantages of circular and continuous motion to enhance the production of a forehand swing, making sure the follow-through went around the neck without stopping. At the time, every coach in the world was still teaching a linear movement—a straight backswing that finished the stroke with the racket pointing at the target.

He tried to explain to me the mathematical principles behind the benefits of perpetual follow-through, scribbling equations on a blackboard in one of our classrooms. Everything he said went completely over my head but I understood what he was getting at when I saw these principles in action. When he was just 12 years old, Jimmy's forehand became a beast, one of the best and most potent weapons at his disposal. His father was, in many ways, the pioneer of the modern stroke. He used his mathematical knowledge to change the game forever.

Jimmy himself has gone on the record about this process, saying, 'My dad wanted me to play tennis and allowed me to be a tennis pro. He was an electrical engineer, so he taught me about physics, and that's how my forehand came about. After my first lesson, he heard the pro giving me all the conventional instruction, and said, "That's the stupidest thing I ever heard in my life. You have to relax your arm and let it go; otherwise, you're slowing the racquet head down; let it fly, and then you'll learn how to hit it in.'"[20]

◆

Beyond knowing what is most important to actively do in order to build a supportive environment for your child and their talent, it is also important to understand what not to do and what kind of behaviours are common in **firecracker** parents that you need to avoid. Be honest with yourself about your own tendencies and learn to recognize toxic traits in yourself and your actions, for example, forcing a child to practise when he does not like the sport as much as you think he does or becoming a full-time know-it-all coach every time you are with your athletic child, putting undue and unnecessary pressure on him at home or in the car, constantly talking about practice and competition, etc.

And another unacceptable thing is to instil guilt and resentment by constantly reminding the young athlete of all the effort and monetary sacrifice that you and the rest of your family have made for him.

Even though some of the best athletes the world has ever known have been raised by parents like this, their greatness is in spite of this behavior not because of it.

Jim Pierce, Mary Pierce's father, was this kind of parent. He loved Mary a lot and while the depth for his affection could not be denied, his entire world revolved around her

---

[20]Arias, Jimmy, 'Jimmy Arias: My Father and Rod Laver', *Tennis.com*, 2 December 2015, https://bit.ly/3DSX7uE. Accessed on 10 February 2023.

tennis. He was obsessed. He would constantly yell at and berate her, losing his temper during practice on a regular basis. He would carry on talking about tennis even after they were off the court, never allowing her a chance to breathe. He would pick fights with people who clapped against her in the stands and created many awkward scenes at practices and real matches alike. He put so much into her and her game; he was never able to separate himself as a parent from himself as part of her training team. As the years wore on, Mary grew more and more frustrated and exhausted. It had lasting effects on her both mentally and emotionally. She ended up firing him when she turned 18. They did not speak for many years. He used to tell me he 'helped build a Ferrari' and that even though he missed her tremendously, he still thought he did the right thing. He and Mary were able to reconcile their relationship before he passed away but it took years and years of turmoil on both ends and a positive outcome was never guaranteed.

Just like how your children should feel comfortable learning and growing from the mistakes they have made, if you make any poor choices, it is your responsibility to change for the betterment of your child and your relationship with them. Serena and Venus Williams's father, Richard Williams, is someone who did just that; he began their early training in one spot and learnt over time where the line was and the difference between what was helping them in an unorthodox way and what was actively harming them. When I first met him, Richard was almost exclusively interested in talking about money and how profitable the sisters could become. He would actively compare them, saying, 'Venus is good, but Serena is the one.'[21]

His coaching style was very different. While the coaches at the academy tended to save technical advice until after the match to prevent overthinking, he would constantly give them technical commands in the middle of sets, telling them to toss the ball higher and other things of that nature. He also did not follow conventional wisdom with regards to training environments. For example, while we believed in the importance of growing in one place in order to reach your fullest potential, Richard was constantly taking the sisters to new places, having them trained by a variety of coaches and dabbling in many different training atmospheres. He would even go as far as to pull them out of matches that they were not going to win to keep them from losing; and he ended up pulling them out of the junior tournament circuit altogether.

The success the sisters have reached proves that some of these techniques have been effective while others haven't; and Richard spent many years learning the best ways to support his daughters. In 2007, during the Sony Ericsson Open, Serena faced Nicole Vaidisova. After losing the first set 6–1, Nicole asked for on-court coaching, which meant that Richard got to go down and coach Serena as well. While Nicole was receiving tactical information, Richard was having a nice and casual chat with his daughter. He praised the outfit she had decided to wear and how well her nails complemented the whole look. He told her that he was enjoying the match and that she should have fun. People laughed, but up in Nicole's box, I was pleasantly

---

[21]This information is based on the author's personal experiences and interactions.

surprised at the kind of growth Richard was showing. His casual approach paid off—Serena easily won the match.

Tommy Haas's father, Peter Haas, is also a good example of a parent who learnt when and how to support their child, and in the process, let them go on to achieve better things. Peter was an experienced coach and an athlete himself so a lot of Tommy's early career was spent under his close and careful guidance. By the time he was 13, as boys of this age often want to do, Tommy wanted independence, wanted to be free from his father's eye and work more with other people. Peter agonized over this decision and he and I had many long conversations about where his son was and where he could go. We knew that Tommy was very mature for his age, often smarter than his peers. Unlike many of them, his insistence on a new coach was not just an adolescent swipe at autonomy but a strategic move to genuinely improve his performance. Peter knew what he had to do and so he did it, despite how hard it was for him. He let Tommy go.

In this way, do not forget that this kind of shift can also happen the other way. A parent's support can deteriorate over time and something that once worked well for a young athlete will not always translate well later on. Yuri Sharapov, Maria Sharapova's father, was that kind of parent—a ferociously dedicated father who helped build a strong supportive environment for his daughter. When she was 13, her workouts became more personalized as we began to really hone in on her strengths and weaknesses and Yuri became more and more involved. I had to meet him before every practice and so we could plan out every detail together—the time, the length of training, the surface, the court number, the coach, the hitting partners and the goals for that particular practice. His input was invaluable and while he expected a lot out of Maria and everyone involved with her training, he always stayed in his lane and was polite, never taking over any of the members' physical responsibilities or blowing up at anyone.

With this kind of commitment, Maria improved steadily and he helped her build on mental and emotional components of her game. As her career continued, Yuri expected more and more from the coaches and while he respected the idea of a team in order to help his daughter improve, he felt the need to control it and to own every aspect of it to ensure its success. Eventually, he began taking her to other coaches in an effort to not only help his daughter's game but to also gain more power over the processes by which she received that help. Despite his concession to delegation, his desire for control over her training and other aspects of her life ended up being too much and tested their relationship. Eventually, Maria wanted more freedom than her father was willing to give her, so their relationship broke down.

◆

Here are some more stories about the parents of famous players as they often are the most illuminating to learn from. Monica Seles and her father, Karolj Seles, had one of the best parent–child relationships that I have ever seen in this sport or any other. They communicated what was appropriate when it was appropriate; and her father knew when to back off and let the rest of her team take the reins and when to step up and guide his daughter in a way he knew only he could. He was a former Olympic athlete himself and had an intimate knowledge and appreciation for my periodization method. He stuck to our plan perfectly, being loyal to the programme while also being flexible as things changed. He was deeply involved in making a lot of the early calls about ways to improve her game, like focussing a lot on maintaining strength and power in the lower body to establish a solid foundation and avoid injury and then began to defer more and more as she grew older.

This level of cooperation is due in large part to a verbal agreement they agreed to very early on that involves following five rules that I think are beneficial to cover here as they provide a clear and concise contract for parents to think about. The entirety of Karolj's coaching ethos was based on these five rules:

1. Respect each other.
2. Tennis is a business.
3. The court is the office.
4. No comments on tennis outside the office.
5. This is her career and not his.

As parents, we are bound to fail our kids in some way. You may not always be able to make and then keep that kind of intense commitment, but you should always be prepared to do the right thing when it matters the most. During the 1992 US Open, Aaron Krickstein was facing Jimmy Connors in the quarterfinals. It was an important match, one that would be replayed over and over again for years to come. Aaron was 24 at the time and in the top 10 of the ATP. Connors, on the other hand, was playing the match on his thirty-ninth birthday and was ranked much lower than Aaron in the top 100. Connors was a beloved player and despite the fact that he would not retire for another 4 years, everyone knew he was on his way out, including Connors himself.

Aaron was ahead by 5–2 in the fifth set. Connors managed to win an incredible point and the tables began to turn. The crowd started cheering him on, excited by the prospect of an underdog comeback from a player who was a decade and a half older than his opponent and on a day that highlighted this stark difference.

Connors became pumped, fuelled by the energy of the crowd and this put pressure on Aaron. He had gotten complacent and was now facing the possibility of a humiliating comeback from Connors if he did not buckle down and end the game. But he was anxious and began to make bad decisions, fault on serves and generally lose his cool. With every mistake that Aaron made, Connors became more confident and emboldened by a crowd hungry to see the seemingly impossible.

Up in the player's box, Dr Krickstein, Aaron's father, was fuming, getting angrier and angrier as his son continued to mess up. He corrected every play under his breath, pleaded with him to get it together and eventually started to promise that he would stop supporting Aaron's athletic career if he lost the match and send him to university where he would only be able to play on a scholarship while majoring in something he was actually good at. In the space of our box, Dr Krickstein proceeded to get more upset than almost any other parent I have ever seen. Back on the court, Aaron just could not get his momentum back and Connors won the match.

After the match was over and Aaron had to face his father, I was sure Dr Krickstein was going to lay into him and further his humiliation by screaming at him and telling him he was done with tennis. To my surprise, Dr Krickstein put a supportive hand on his son's shoulder and told him that this match would help them make sure that something like this did not happen again. He asked Aaron what he could learn from this experience and they walked off talking strategy together, humbled but excited. Dr Krickstein was able to control his emotions and separate his more irrational responses from what he knew his son needed from him. The father–son duo came out of a bad situation stronger than ever. What people often do not know about Aaron is that, after his loss to Connors, he went on to win 10 Grand Slam comebacks down two sets to love, which tied him for an Open Era record. His father's composure had a powerful effect on his gameplay for the rest of his career.

Being a supportive parent for a talented child in any field is tough but the rigours of sports provide a specific challenge, in so much that physical development often overshadows the relational elements that need to be established early on for any kind of growth to be possible. Failure, like success, is not a static state of being for anybody; it is constantly shifting and changing, giving you avenues to earn new things. Do the internal work to understand the weight of all your choices, the ways in which your actions and attitudes affect the dynamic you have with your child but do not be afraid to fail as a parent. Only through failure can we learn what works best and continue to adapt to what our child needs.

20

COACHING

I will cut straight to the chase—the core principle of being a good coach is sacrifice. This manifests itself in a variety of ways but at the end of the day, the first step to becoming a good coach is to understand that the success of your athletes is both about you and your commitment to the job and also not about you at all.

This paradigm might seem a little confusing to some, especially young coaches who are new to the industry and eager to turn their students into world-renowned champions but if you never come to understand this dynamic, you only limit yourself and the athletes you work with. You, as the coach, have a unique and invaluable perspective that the athlete cannot possess but that same position is also what allows you to only be able to guide and steer your player. The things you bring to an athlete's game are vital but it is not about you. This also means taking the blame; you experience all the pressure of being the face of the operation without getting any of the credit. Or, put more simply, when the athlete wins it is because of he athlete's prowess but when the athlete loses, the coach is bad.

Coaches are never singularly great figures of vast and superior knowledge of their craft. The best coaches are constantly reading books, listening to talks, attending conferences, absorbing advice and information pioneered and made available by other coaches. This takes a level of humility. Being cocky and overconfident about what you know (or, perhaps more accurately, what you think you know) not only does a disservice to the progression of your players but also to yourself. The only way that coaches can grow and learn, thereby allowing their players to do the same, is to implement and improve upon the ever-expanding foundations of what has come before them. A respect for your elders and those who are more experienced than you is absolutely necessary, more so than other fields.

The most crucial choice a parent can make in their child's life is to select a suitable coach. No matter how good or experienced the coach is, they must believe in the child's talent and potential. Otherwise, the relationship never works. Coaches have a responsibility to establish a special connection, a bond of genuine trust with their athletes to work on their intellect, behaviour, practices, beliefs, values and feelings, not only in the realm of their sport but their entire life. Again, experience and ability count for nothing if there is no relationship between the student and the mentor based on 100 per cent commitment.

The most effective coaches are the ones who not only understand their student's goals and aspirations from day one but who also actively reciprocate that ambition by letting their students know exactly what it is that can be gained or expected from their instruction. Communication is key. Coaches should promote self-learning and mutual accountability as they work with their students towards the same goal. This also applies to focus. Coaches of young athletes are focussed on the future, while coaches of pro-athletes concentrate more on current results.

Simply put, a coach who seeks out credit for himself cannot succeed. As previously mentioned, the best coaches are giving and humble, avoiding the limelight so that others can shine. The coaches that have their athlete's best interest as the foundation of their training do not care what other people think about them. They are totally committed to making champions and achieving their goal of excellence. In this way, coaches and athletes are very similar.

Coaches need to understand the difference between coaching and teaching to be most effective. A coach's job is not to tell the students what to do but to explain how to do it; the process is more active. Coaches are responsible not just for technical skill or mechanical knowledge but also for the entire process of implementation and execution, both inside and outside of the student's field of passion. Going all the way back to Chapter 11, all the knowledge in the world means nothing if it cannot be communicated and used properly. A coach's responsibility is to guide their athlete towards finding the lessons within themselves, encouraging introspection and self-discovery rather than blindly following the orders of some arbitrary outside force. Coaches often utilize questions in a manner akin to the Socratic method, through inquiry meant to draw out, inspect, and change underlying assumptions and ideas: Why did you make that decision and was it the right one? What did you learn? What did you do correctly and what can you do better?

Similarly, coaches are in a unique position in an athlete's life. They do not have the emotional attachment of parents but they also do not have the authoritarian image of an instructor (ideally), so they are allowed to navigate an athlete's internal struggles from a different perspective. This allows them to take an athlete and their game to another level.

Another aspect of a coach's job that may seem counterproductive at first is the irrevocable march toward greatness that almost always leads to the athlete outgrowing the coach's training. All the greats have worked with multiple coaches over the span of their careers because they have had to. The guidance they require changes over time because their skills and need change over time. If coaches do their job correctly, then the players they mentor should inevitably outgrow them. This is what coaches strive for.

Building on this last point, parents are not the only ones who need to know when to let their players go, even if it means giving up the professional game altogether. When one of my students, a Brazilian player who ranked at No. 30 in the world junior rankings, turned 18, we had a long and deep conversation about his future. He had just gotten a scholarship to play at Harvard; and as much as he wanted to play professional tennis, we both knew that Harvard was a once-in-a-lifetime opportunity. His departure filled me with joy because I knew that it was the best thing for him.

◆

Another aspect of coaching, and leadership in general, that is usually misunderstood, especially by those who are inexperienced, is that trust is a gift and respect is earned. On top of believing in an athlete's ability to achieve their goals, a coach has to prove their worth and their chops through actions. They need to show the person they are training why they deserve to be a part of this journey and have this sort of relationship with the athletes. This is a kind of negotiation, a give and take. You have to be willing to put the work in to develop a dynamic with the athlete that leads to respect and genuine fondness. Things like fear, authority and obligation—these are forces that may get you some decent results early on but will quickly erode any kind of longevity the relationship can have because they are not earned but demanded.

This is why quality coaching requires sacrifices, even and especially when you do not want to make them. My schedule with my athletes starts at six in the morning and goes until late in the evening for seven days a week. I have missed plenty of meals, trips and holiday celebrations with my own family because I was busy training athletes. This is not some surprise disruption; it is a normal and natural part of my job, one that my family has learnt to adapt to. This is the kind of commitment it takes to earn and keep deep-seated trust between coaches and their players.

There is, however, a kind of balance and consideration that this level of commitment requires, in so much that when you are training more than one athlete, you need to devote yourself to each of them in a way that does not show favouritism. You cannot operate in a way that can sow discord between athletes and disrupt their mental fortitude.

For example, when Agassi and Courier were playing against one another in the finals of the 1991 French Open, I decided to go to Champs-Élysées to watch the match on TV rather than pick a spot at the stadium. Nick Bollettieri never understood my preoccupation with showing equal support and so he went to watch the game from Agassi's box, effectively cheering against Courier even though he appreciated him too. Courier was disappointed to see Nick in the opposite box; and despite winning the match, he left the academy shortly after that. Nick still did not learn his lesson. When Boris Becker showed up to the academy, wanting to reclaim his No.1 spot in the ATP, Nick dropped everything, including Agassi, to coach him, despite the fact that he had no history of chemistry with Becker at all. Of course, Agassi was furious and did not speak to him for many years. It should be obvious that this is not a good strategy to follow if your goal is to create strong, authentic bonds with your athletes.

This feeds into another aspect of coaching, one that is less interesting than the others. Namely, your job as a coach is to also manage the other people that make up your player's team. As a coach, there is an entire dimension of your job dedicated to fulfilling bureaucratic duties such as making sure that everyone on the team is satisfied in a way that allows the whole unit to operate properly. Sometimes, that means chasing after disaffected athletes and convincing them to come back for the sake of their careers and working as a sort of interpersonal conflict mediator to get things back on track. You have to be able to wear different hats as you deal with different kinds of people, while keeping the greater good of your athlete at the heart of every decision.

The heart and soul of coaching is commitment and investment, giving your all to prepare your students for everything that they will face. However, this also means knowing when to step back and let your students take responsibility for their own actions, letting them learn when and how to take matters into their own hands. Finding a balance between these two approaches is as difficult as it is rewarding.

A coach on my team was the best at achieving this kind of balance. He knew when to be in the front and when to hang back. Once, during the US Open, he was conducting the match from the coaches' box and his pupil was losing and getting frustrated. He finally broke down and yelled at him to guide him in some way. The coach responded coolly to the heat, telling his pupil to go up to the net after a wide serve. He did and started playing a little better before more unforced errors stopped the momentum he had been building in its tracks, which cost him more points. Again, the player exploded at his coach, asking him to shut up, but the coach never wavered. He knew his tactics had been the right ones. So, while his student continued to rage, the coach sat there, calm and smiling, telling himself that it was clear that his player had let his nerves get the better of him.

This game was televized and many people criticized the coach's style. Did he not care how he was treated? Where was his pride? But he stood his ground; he did not care what people thought. This was a matter between him and his player. That is another kind of sacrifice that you must be willing to make as a coach—to do the unpopular thing when you know it is best for your players.

But, again, there is another element of balance here. Being too involved and obsessed with your image can damage your student's self-perception, even if your intention is good. This is something that young coaches struggle with a lot and I was no exception. Once, I warmed up with one of my students during an ATP tournament. I was younger then and was still playing points and sets. When we finished, another player came up to me and asked if I could help him warm-up as well, to which I gladly agreed. Since I did not know any better, I only cared about myself; I did not even consider that I was warming up a player going through moments of doubt in his sports career. He asked me to play a few points and I ran with the score, easily winning most of the games.

On the court next to ours, Guillermo Vilas was practising with Ion Tiriac, his coach, and probably the best coach in the world. Seeing our warm-up set, Ion came up to me and asked me whether I was a player or a coach. I told him that I was a coach and that it was an honour to meet him. I held out my hand in greeting but he didn't shake it; instead, he just stared at me. He proceeded to give me a lecture that I will never forget. He told me that if it was true that I was a trainer, then I did not know what the hell I was doing and that clearly, my priorities were out of order. He told me that coaching is not about the coach; it is about the player. 'All these people you see around here have come to see him, not you. Your job is to give confidence to the player. Wake up.' He turned and walked away before I could respond.

As harsh as his words were, he was right. At that point in my career, I barely understood the true nature of what it meant to be a coach, let alone what it took to get there. Indeed, my maneouver had filled that young player with uncertainty and he ended up losing his match in the tournament. Nevertheless, it was a jolt of reality that I desperately needed. It was one of the most important moments in my entire career.

Coaching is not an easy job, but every aspect of a coach's responsibilities is vital to the success of their athletes.

Becoming a good coach is not something that happens overnight; rather, much like an athlete's own journey, it is something that you grow into. You gain and hone a set of skills, intuition and experiences over time. It is not about being a perfect coach but being the best coach that you can be for the athlete, the best version of yourself.

21

TEAM AND ENVIRONMENT

There is a famous African proverb that posits that 'it takes a village to raise a child'. It means that the upbringing and development of a child is not the sole responsibility of a person, set of parents or household; every member of the community is equally responsible for that child. This might seem like something of an antiquated understanding of child rearing, especially with how much emphasis is placed on upholding tightly–knit familial relationships, especially in the US, but this idea is as relevant as ever and doubly so for the field of elite sports.

Most people tend to think of famous sports stars, musicians, writers and artists as singularly great figures that were born as brilliant as they appear. This is especially true if the artist is not a part of a band or group of some kind but a singular person doing something by themselves. They see the one person singing or acting or hitting the ball and they assume this one person is the only person responsible for their success.

As we have established, this is totally false but the depths of how inaccurate this is, especially in the world of tennis and other elite single-player sports, are often overlooked, even by those that claim to know the complexities. Take

Kei Nishikori as an example. He had, in addition to his entire family, a sponsor, a liaison to the sponsor, a manager, a translator, a head coach, multiple hitting partners, a strength coach, a conditioning coach, a kinesiologist, a psychologist, a school advisor as well as several teachers, a public speaking coach, a travel specialist and a nutritionist; all helping him achieve his highest potential in various areas of his gameplay and career, adapting and working together, playing off one another for his benefit. This is just one player, who is not even on the level of an Agassi, a Woods or a Bolt.

Another important but widely forgotten factor that contributes to a player's success is their partnership with their peers and fellow athletes. Training is no more a singular activity than the game itself is. A player needs an opponent, someone to strive against and to work off of. I have seen relationships blossom into lifelong friendships at the academy, which is why fostering a community of mutual respect and support, even among competing athletes, is so important.

We have examples of famous, highly competitive establishments that boast of having some of the world's most recognized players and top-notch coaching staff. But as it turns out, none of it matters. Despite being incredibly talented, the coaching staff has no sense of community or continuity in their actions. They constantly give contradictory instructions, misspeak and undermine the authority of their peers behind each other's backs and ignore each other, to the students' confusion. It is impossible to know whom to follow or what to do in this work environment.

We can learn many valuable lessons from such organizations that have this kind of hostile environment.

First, all members have to agree on the system and methodology of training, understanding that everyone is equally important to the team. This allows the group to work together toward the same goal. Second, parents need to be aware of these environments, which could be detrimental to the student's progress.

A pivotal practice to instil is having 15 to 30 minute meetings daily with the team before going out on the field. You can start with small talk, make jokes and get to know each other better before talking about business—the goals for the day, what needs immediate attention, things the athletes are doing well in and the things they can improve in. Parents, coaches and athletes need to build this dynamic and intimate camaraderie as soon as possible. These few-minute meetings are critical for creating a stable and harmonious working environment.

A classic visual metaphor I would often employ with the younger students is that of a bundle of sticks. I would take them outside and instruct them to find and break a stick. Easy, right? Then, I would then ask them to gather a whole bunch of sticks, maybe 10 or 12, and try to break them while holding them as one large bundle. Even if the sticks they had found were little more than small twigs, the bundle proved to be nearly impossible to break when they were put all together. The message is obvious—there is strength in numbers.

There is another more obscure way of thinking about this principle that adds a bit of nuance. Consider the Portuguese man-of-war a beautiful aquatic creature that is one of my favourite animals. It looks and acts a lot like a jellyfish, with stinging tentacles drifting from a floating top but it is technically what biologists call a 'siphonophore' or a colonial organism, meaning that it is actually 4 genetically distinct organisms that have combined and adapted over time to operate as one larger creature. Each part of the Portuguese man-of-war is a distinct being with a distinct function but these parts cannot survive on their own. They have evolved to work together in order to survive. One organism is the floating top, a little bubble-like membrane with a fin (spiked and reminiscent of the sails of the boat it gets its name from) that turns and moves in order to manipulate waves and wind patterns, to move since the creature itself cannot actually swim. The second organism acts as its digestive system, giving nutrients to the other parts of itself. The third organism is responsible for reproduction, changing practical function depending on whether or not it is male or female. The fourth organism controls the tentacles, which the man-of-war drags behind as it floats, that stretch to lengths upwards of 160 ft, trapping and killing various fish as prey.

The point of this bizarre biological tangent should be obvious. In the world of excellence, passion, talent and becoming the best in the world, we arrive at our dreams by working together. We work together not just to survive but to thrive, with each of us having a place in the life and career of an athlete and bringing something vital to the table. A true team leader works with the members of the athlete's team to figure out how they can best serve the team's goal and strives to cultivate a climate of true connection.

This connection is not one that can afford to stay strictly professional. Like I mentioned in earlier chapters, the heart and soul of training an elite athlete is commitment and this means going above and beyond for your staff and co-workers in ways that would be more appropriate for family members because, realistically, that is what they are set to become if you do your job correctly. A poignant example of such commitment is a young Colombian coach who was at the core of Anna Kournikova's team and a major reason for a lot of her success on the court. He was diagnosed with Lou Gehrig's Disease after years of being her main hitter during practice. He lost all ability to move his body in spite of his mind still being sharp. The coach was staying at one of the apartments at the academy when he found out he needed to go back to Colombia to receive proper treatment and be with his family. He needed a private flight since his condition made it so that he could not fly on commercial airlines. Without any hesitation or prompting from anyone else, Kournikova paid for his flight and all the bills associated with getting him settled back home. This was never a question for her or something that she had to think about. She did it out of the kindness of her heart and, perhaps more centrally, an understanding of her coach as part of her family and her innermost circle. This is not an uncommon bond to have developed.

This next story has multiple lessons. When I was 15, my mother brought me along to the World Coaches Conference, which is a gathering some of the best coaching talents on the planet. She was presenting there. I was beginning to get into the world of sports and coaching but was confused by the prevalence of the terms like 'mine' when coaches referred to their students. There was something possessive and unnecessary about using such terms of ownership. I asked my mom about this trend and she, never one to miss out on the potential for a teachable moment, told me to go around to the booths of various famous coaches and ask for their answer. I have never been a particularly anxious or shy person, so I did just that. Every answer was some variation of this idea of family. These coaches became so invested in their players and their co-workers that it was not a matter of possession for them but of complete devotion. They were committed in the deepest way, often spending more time with their athletes and teams than with their own kids. I learnt that this was the price of greatness—this kind of relationship was the foundation of absolute coaching.

◆

We have discussed the individual members of a player's team and we have discussed the importance of a strong dynamic between said individuals but something that often gets overlooked is the general atmosphere that needs to be created and sustained in order to properly develop any kind of elite-level talent; and people and their relationships are a part of it, but only a part.

If you look back at any movement of great artists throughout history, many of them were involved in a tight-knit community of other artists along with whom they were able to build an ecology of brilliance. Think of folks like Langston Hughes, Zora Neale Hurston and Louis Armstrong during the Harlem Renaissance, Raphael, Leonardo Da Vinci and Michelangelo during the Italian Renaissance; François Truffaut, Jean-Luc Godard and Éric Rohmer during the French New Wave of Cinema, etc. These were not just some arbitrary groups of people that future historians bundled together in order to give some flimsy continuity to past events. These people knew each other and had relationships, both personal and professional, that allowed them to thrive.

This kind of interpersonal dynamic does not happen in a vacuum; the central access of a shared location fosters a creative environment. Florence, Paris, Harlem—it may seem obvious, but sharing a space is vital to the process. Not only because it helps stoke that sense of community and shared striving toward greatness but also because that kind of group relationship helps stimulate and influence the wider areas around them. This is how you create a cultural nexus.

We can think about this beyond the scope of individuals. Creating a nexus imbues whatever the specific place is with the essence of that thing, affecting future industry and future talent. Hollywood and movies, Silicon Valley and tech companies, Boca Chica in the Dominican Republic and baseball, Florida and tennis—these places will always, to a greater or lesser degree, be associated with these things because of the kind of opportunities they have provided and continue to provide to people. It is not enough to have a 'scene'; any town or state can have a local scene or a minor hotspot of interest in a particular field. They may even produce one or two local legends. Rather, it is more about establishing a more widespread view of talent, where one is synonymous with the best of the best.

This leads us to the often overlooked brass tacks reality of this kind of community building. If you want to foster this kind of success, it requires resources that are not available to everyone. We will get more into this in the next section when we talk about the business end of a lot of these principles, but for the time being, understand that, similar to what I discussed in Chapter 1 about talent being a seed that needs to be developed and made to sprout over time, access to adequate resources, both financial and otherwise, is most definitely a key to that process. The most talented athletes the world has ever known would have gotten nowhere without the proper foresight and environmental support of wealthy figures in the industry.

Because the vast majority of the best athletes have to be scouted and recruited, this means that for parents looking to give their children the best shot possible at becoming a champion, the academies and camps they look into should be only the best of the best and should be looking into attracting the best talent in order to maintain that legacy. For parents, it may seem like something of a chicken or the egg sort of paradox that your child needs talent to get talent. But this is much less of a barrier than it sounds like, at least beyond financial hurdles. With dutiful research, sacrifice and proper support, a child's talent can be developed via these nexuses.

This is the same principle that is behind various fellowships, residencies and programmes that are available to artists and writers at various universities. When all is said and done, it is simply not possible to achieve anything past a certain threshold of excellence without being constantly immersed in this kind of environment, surrounded by people who get it, who know your ambitions and have their own, who know the ins and outs of the industry and are learning the nuances with you. It is not possible to grow past a certain point without this kind of deep connection to the people and resources around you in these kinds of unique environments.

Many high-performance institutes essentially operate as farm teams or practice squads, places where young players get the opportunity to work with and train under high-profile athletes and coaches in order to gain unprecedented knowledge and experience. This reveals something else about the process of building these kinds of communities—they are constructed out of people but are also the people themselves. Everything that makes these kinds of nexuses great is born out of two things—the specific resources and circumstances of a place and the people of that place. This is why nepotism is such a big problem in so many fields as it all comes down to people.

Such communities can be found all over the world but only the best and brightest allow a talented athlete to become a champion. These kinds of connections and the principles gained from them are integral to the success of talented young people in any field and it is up to parents to work with coaches and other members of a child's support system to find the best communities for their children.

22

SPONSORS

An undeniable fact of pursuing any passion at an elite level is the financial burden that is placed on the child and their family, especially in the early stages. Every industry, whether it be musical, literary, artistic or athletic, is different; requires an understanding of different nuances of how money plays a role in the success of an up-and-coming star and vice versa. This chapter, of course, focusses largely on the ins and outs of tennis but the first core principle for parents to understand about this aspect of their child's future is that research is an absolute must. As with the investigation of the best camps and academies in your area, understanding not just the 'how' but also the 'why' of sponsorship is invaluable for your child's future, no matter their field. Ask questions, get involved and learn about the industry.

The first thing to understand is the general timeline of monetary assistance. Athletes do not generally get any kind of deal or contract until the age of 12 or 13. This is for multiple reasons. Firstly, as we have established in this book's first section, these tend to be the years that burnouts/dropouts are mostly prominent and likely, meaning that an investment in an athlete, no matter how promising in the earliest stages of their career, is not favourable, since so much is bound to change in the teenage years. An investment is all about tracking kinetic energy and about reading patterns and trends in order to make the right call. At the end of the day, that is what any kind of sponsorship is. It is an investment in the future based on the player's current ability and potential. This is another reason why you need to do your research early on. Parents need to be armed with knowledge in order to make the best deals while they are in charge of their children's finances.

The first round of financial aid that is available to athletes at this point in their career are training scholarships—relatively small amounts of money that usually, like the name would suggest, cover training and give severe discounts on equipment costs. These scholarships do not assist with schooling or any other general aid. This stage is, in many ways, the most dependent on raw skill as this aid allows the athlete to move onto the next plateau in their career and make the one after that more accessible and so on and so forth.

Around the age of 15, small deals with certain manufacturers start becoming available. The deals are usually around $50,000 plus coverage for equipment exclusive to that manufacturer. For someone who is unfamiliar with the ins and outs of the industry, this can seem like a lot of money but in the grand scheme of things, it is really just seed money. See, at this stage of their career, between 13 and 17, an athlete should not only be dominating the junior rankings but also begin to dabble in the challenger circuit to enter the professional world. This is not really enough to make a living off of, especially with all the travel that goes into merely attending various professional events.

This is a very rough number, but on an average, the life of a touring athlete at this stage will cost $2,000 a week and these athletes play for (again, on an average) 10 weeks a year. The way most players are able to afford this kind of expense at this point in their career is through donors. Nick Bollettieri will go down in history as one of the greatest coaches of all time. One of his greatest attributes was raising money with his wealthy friends to finance the career of young promising athletes. These donors are incredibly wealthy, sports-loving individuals who help promising young athletes in the hopes that they will become the next superstars. Unfortunately, large companies that are willing to give the money and attention needed to boost a small handful of specific athletes are few and far between.

This is, again, where research and accurate industry knowledge comes into play. Not just because you need to know the National Collegiate Athletic Association (NCAA) guidelines for accepting money from a donor to keep their eligibility above board but also because an athlete's guardians are the ones legally in charge of their financial decisions and legal contracts until they turn 18. Often, the very real need for financial relief can lead to an impatience that can end up wrecking your child's future. Both athletes and their parents have to be smart about the choices they make, especially when so much is on the line.

For example, I advise parents to never take any money in a deal based on future earnings. This may seem obvious but I have seen such impatience ruin the financial standing of great athletes, many of whom did not have the chance to speak for themselves. Not only do you never know what is going to happen in the future and cannot guarantee the performance of athletes at such a transitional stage but also that deal can turn into a loan depending on future performance. When the athlete earns enough money, sponsors and investors offer funds. The amount depends on the mutually agreed upon percentage by the parents and the investor. Sponsors can cover all sorts of sports-related revenue—prize money, exhibitions, endorsements, etc. If the call is not met inside a certain period, the backer has the right to demand a return of their money often with high interest; and if the athlete is not getting paid enough to pay off the loan in the first place, then they are almost certainly not going to be able to pay off the loan once they have defaulted. It is a horrible situation to be in and is never worth the momentary relief. This is also why I never recommend using personal finances or property security for loans either.

Mark McCormack, founder of IMG (earlier known as International Management Group), was a visionary who saw the potential endorsement opportunities in the increasingly widespread reach of TV broadcasting. He was a lawyer, an agent and an author, and before his death in 2003, he worked with countless athletes to get them the representation they deserved. I got to work with him on multiple occasions after IMG bought out the academy and he had this business philosophy that he would always remind me of when he was in the midst of making any kind of legal agreement. He always said that some deals were as easy as a firm handshake but others were much more difficult and took much more time and patience. Being a good business person and having a sound financial mind is all about patience, about knowing when to go all in and when to hang back and try a different tactic. This is the mindset that I would like parents to have when it comes to their kid's financial future in any sport. You are in control of signing contracts and making momentous decisions, so you need to resist the urge to act on impulse and instead act on logical thought and careful consideration.

It is worth noting here that single-player sports, like tennis, golf, swimming and gymnastics, have a unique track compared to other games like pro basketball or football, since the university path is entirely separate from the professional one in this case. This is another choice players and parents have to make. In individual sports, for an athlete who decides to play for a university, continuing the professional athletic quest takes longer than their counterparts' who turn pro after their senior year. But till today, those athletes can see a ifferent level of fame and financial success. The NCAA guidelines keep each avenue separate; the young athletes can receive incredibly robust and generous financial aid packages for said education, room and board. More and more athletes are attending college first and turning pro later and it is a highly recommended way to proceed.

There is a classic IMG story about how Tiger Woods first got signed. After winning 18 straight match play victories in 1996 and becoming the undisputed best amateur of this era, Tiger wanted to go pro. His father, Earl Woods, handled every aspect of his career at this point and met with a team of agents and executives from IMG to discuss a possible contract. They all gathered in New York City, with all the different departments organizing top-tier presentations to wow him. They explained every facet of their proposal in great detail. The agent, who represented Tiger, would only work for him. Next, marketing experts explained the strong possibility of endorsements from brands like Nike. Then, the company's business leaders walked him through the ins and outs of starting not only a quality brand but an eventual empire; a business model that would only grow and expand in popularity and profit as Tiger got better and better.

In spite of all the efforts put in by the organization, Tiger's father fell asleep early on during the pitch. No one wanted to be the one to wake him up since they felt that he would assume this move was more confrontational than it was and take his business elsewhere, so the majority of the presentation was given to an unconscious audience. Once it was over and Earl finally woke up, all he did was ask 'When do we start?' while rubbing sleep out of his eyes. While this is a funny story, Earl was familiar with the presentation's content ahead of time. You should always study ahead to be prepared when dealing with potential business partnerships and their effects on you and your family.

Money is certainly a huge factor in the choices a parent and their child have to make but it should not be the only thing being considered. Ultimately, your skills and connections can get your further than any number of zeroes at the end of a cheque can. I mean this very pragmatically—contracts with firms and other managing companies can often lead to a more general career boost, which provides things like wild cards for tournaments that you may not be able to enter otherwise or the connections with a good team expediting the trajectory of your overall career. This is especially true if the athlete is from an affluent family and has the financial resources to cover the early costs of their athletic career, since, in that case, the most valuable thing to these athletes is access to a top-notch institute and a training programme that allows them to reach their full potential. Of course, not everyone is in this kind of a position, but the point is that money is not the only important element in an athlete's career; as a parent, you need to think more holistically than that.

When all is said and done, nothing is more important than maintaining and improving an athlete's gameplay. Kei, when he was only 17 years old and just beginning to enter the challenger circuit, got an incredibly tempting offer for a sponsorship. Kei had a small standing contract with Wilson rackets, which covered equipment plus $50,000 a year. A spokesperson for Prince, a rival racket manufacturer, offered Kei $1,000,000 a year to endorse their brand.

There are no brands that are of better or worse quality; they are just better or worse for the tendencies and habits of certain players. It is hard to make a switch in your equipment, especially when you have trained with a certain type of racket for the entirety of your formative tennis life. We set up a whole variety of stations on the court, every inch of the sidelines filled with rackets of all shapes and sizes, strung with different materials and to various degrees of tightness. Kei hit and hit and hit; he played points, sets and sometimes full matches, experimenting and collecting data. The next day, Kei came into my office, torn about what he should do. None of the Prince rackets had felt exactly right, but none of them had felt off either; he could try to adjust to them. Besides, he was finding it hard to turn down the chance to make more than 20 times his current salary. I told him that tennis was his business and that it should thus be treated with absolute care and seriousness. It was ultimately his choice, but I advised him that the money was not worth suffering a string of losses. With Prince, he would make a million dollars, but with Wilson, he would go on to make millions. A few days later, he turned down the offer and later went on to prove me right.

This advice is aimed squarely at the young athletes—as confusing and alien as a lot of this sponsorship stuff can seem in the moment, especially when it comes to the abstract reality of finances, it behooves you to develop an appreciation for what is going on in this facet of your career at an early age. Put more simply, do not be too harsh or dismissive towards your parents or your agents. They truly are here to help you become the greatest athlete you can be. I had the chance to catch up with Jim Courier and he stressed on the importance of maintaining good relationship with your agents and sponsors, saying:

> One thing I've learnt over the years is [sponsors] are your partners and you need to be aware of what they're interested in and what they're trying to gain from their association with you and you need to try and help them... We have so many good examples these days of players who spend a lot of time with their corporate partners to make sure they're getting what they need out of these relationships and it's mutually beneficial... You really can benefit from working in a very symbiotic relationship with your corporate partners and help them achieve their goals too... Just be mindful that you need to help them too and carve a little bit of time out of your schedule to make things better for them because that will pay off in the long-term and keep those relationships longer and everyone will win.[22]

---

[22]This information is based on the author's personal interactions.

This part of the process can be frustrating and hard to navigate, for both parents and students, but like many other aspects of the life led by elite athletes, the key is to do your research, to not allow yourself to be blinded by greed or short-term gains and to always do what is best for the careers of everyone involved.

23

MARKETING

Another aspect of elite athleticism that is tied to sponsorship is the athlete's marketability. An athlete's ability to attract endorsement deals and gain public support is extremely important. However, for some reason, marketability is not talked about very often. It seems like most coaching books and how-to guides assume that this is a natural side effect of talent or exposure. This is simply not true. A player's appeal, like any other skill, is something that needs to be honed and worked on constantly. An athlete's marketability is baked into every aspect of their life—their gameplay, sportsmanship, interview skills and public speaking ability, the kinds of things they get up to off the court, their views on current events, their online presence, etc.

In many ways, marketability has very little to do with someone's athletic ability. The sport may be how people are first introduced to you, but for athletes that manage to reach a truly transcendent status, it is never the only component to their success. Serena Williams is an icon of American Blackness and a symbol of the power of womanhood and motherhood, even for those who have no interest in tennis. You can take a selfie with a Roger Federer hologram as soon as you get off the plane at Zurich airport. Michael Phelps is not only the best swimmer of all time but is also the face of the sport across the world, as most people cannot even name another professional swimmer. This extends into financial success as well, not just notoriety.[23] Only $90 million of Michael Jordan's estimated $2.1 billion came from National Basketball Association (NBA) earnings. That is the difference between being a champion and being a star.

That kind of status is all about marketability and marketability is all about reach. Athletes are in a prime position for fame like no one else. They have the chance to go beyond their calling and become entities entirely divorced from their original context. Consider the kind of influence sports have on virtually every culture. Even people who do not care about sports watch the Olympics; and the World Cup in 2018 was watched by 3.5 billion people, making it the most watched thing to ever be shown on TV.[24]

There is not necessarily a step-by-step guide or rule book that teaches you to make yourself more marketable and influential since a lot of the cumulative weight of the public persona is made up of a lot of unique minute-to-minute situations. The strategy that an athlete and their team choose to implement will vary wildly, depending largely on habits and tendencies both on and off the court as well as on a deep understanding of the athlete's individual preferences.

[23]David, Juan Paolo, 'What is Michael Jordan's Net Worth as of February 2023? Exploring His Airness' Business Empire', *Sportskeeda*, 17 February 2023, https://tinyurl.com/54k4x4vs. Accessed on 20 February 2023.
[24]'More than Half of the World Watched Record-Breaking 2018 World Cup', FIFA, 21 December 2018, https://tinyurl.com/2ckhzzr6 Accessed on 20 February 2023.

Whatever the angle, an athlete should never be flippant about the impact they can have, be dismissive about interactions with the press and other players or miss an opportunity to build their public image. This is where capitalistic business terminology comes in. Many of these instances are chances to reinforce a personal brand and should be taken seriously. This includes 'brand management' online—on places like Instagram and Twitter—where every action, comment and mistake is scrutinized and amplified.

What we are really talking about here is legacy. How is the world going to remember you as an athlete, as a celebrity and as a person? It is important to take this matter seriously as the only thing more harmful to an athlete's legacy than having a middling relationship with the public is having a bad reputation—whether it's because people find you difficult to work with, see you as actively antagonistic towards your opponents or witness you engaging in unprofessional behaviour. The classic adage of there 'being no such thing as bad publicity' is simply and fundamentally incorrect, especially in these kinds of situations. It should surprise no one that being a marketing nightmare is not a good marketing strategy.

For the record, I am not referring to adopting a kind of rebel or punk effect. As counterintuitive and ironic as it may seem, that kind of anti-establishment aesthetic can be tremendously popular and we have seen many people, and movements who have adopted that style gain fame and support. No, what I am talking about is dysfunctionality and the reputation that inevitably comes with it. If you look at someone like, say, Lindsay Lohan, it does not matter how many well-received movies she's in, how much money she makes or how many projects she undertakes, even the ones outside of film, like her TV career, management positions and modelling. All that matters to the general public are the stories about her addiction-related breakdowns in the late 2000s and how famously hard she is to work with, all of which lead to her earning the title of a 'diva'. There are a lot of factors to this widespread perception (sensationalized reporting, burgeoning meme culture that grew as the internet did and general entertainment industry misogyny), but this stigma around her persists, to the point where the only real way to gain traction with the public is through ironic appreciation. Most people only talk about and engage with Lohan to hate on her and talk smack about her, and her public image needs to play into that. This is how you wind up with things like *Lindsay Lohan's The Price of Fame*, an officially licensed mobile game that centred around gaining fans by being involved in increasingly ridiculous scandals.

This is a position you never want to be in. You want the public to be on your side, through the highs and lows of your career. Of course, every popular person is going to have haters and detractors, but there's a difference between getting hate in a way that clearly stems from jealousy and only elevates you and hate that genuinely takes away from your public image. Every member of an athlete's support team needs to be attuned to the needs of the particular athlete that they work with to bolster their image as much as they can. The athlete needs to have enough self-awareness to carve out their brand, both on the inside and the outside. This process can look similar between various athletes but is more often than not caused by totally different circumstances that are unique to that player. For example,

Maria Sharapova and Kei Nishikori were students of mine who needed to improve their public speaking skills. For Maria, it was all about tonality and miscommunication. She tried to be confident and self-assured but kept coming off as arrogant and rude in all her early press appearances, so she had to learn how to properly convey what she was trying to say and Kei knew that his chances of becoming a major tennis star were virtually zero if he did not learn how to speak English fluently, so he had an entirely different set of public speaking challenges to overcome.

Basically, marketability is all about identifying your strengths and weaknesses as a player and a person and leaning into an angle that gives you not only the farthest reach possible but also the most opportunities to flex your specific specialties. Perhaps the most well-known example of effective marketing in the tennis world is that of Anna Kournikova, mainly because her presence in the wider popular culture was not really tied to her tennis skills.

Anna's mother recognized the importance of good marketing. She knew that her daughter fit into the popular beauty standards, so she taught her to lean into that. When Anna was 12 or 13, she began to wear clothing that was more revealing than conventional tennis outfits. It was not just her physical appearance that was being showcased, since marketing someone based on their perceived attractiveness works best in tandem with the idea that the celebrity also has an alluring personality. Anna was taught early on how to interact with crowds, smiling and flirting in a way that further bolstered her brand and made her seem more appealing to fans without turning her into a one-note caricature. She had to juggle her physical and mental well-being, the misogynistic celebrity culture and the need to counter the constant focus on her looks through improved gameplay. It was a fine line to walk but one that she walked admirably. She would often have larger crowds show up to watch her practice; she had to know how to navigate that attention without sacrificing the benefits of the practice. For several years during the height of her career, she was always one of the most Googled people in the world, especially via Google image search.

Many people look back over her 12-year tennis career and conclude that Kournikova was never that good of a player, mainly because she never won a WTA singles title and was 'only' world No. 8 in women's singles. I happen to think that Kournikova was a much better player than people give her credit for and that a lot of that dismissal is based in misogyny—she was subjected to constant objectification and sexualization in the broader culture (ESPN ranked her the 'hottest female athlete' of all time in 2011 while also ranking her No. 18 in the '25 worst sports flops' only seven years earlier while her career was still going on). People often forget that Kournikova reached No. 1 in women's doubles with Martina Hingis and won 16 titles—achievements that cannot be scoffed at.

In many ways, however, the question of whether Anna was good at tennis somewhat irrelevant because the fact is that being the best tennis player in the world was never really the long-term goal of her or her team. Tennis ended up being more of a springboard that led to one of the most prolific and successful careers of an athlete outside sports of all time. Some of the opportunities were linked directly to her appearance, like the photo shoots she did for *Maxim*,

FHM and *Sports Illustrted*. However, she also did a slew of endorsements and exhibitions, landed minor film roles, hosted a season of *The Biggest Loser*, became an ambassador for a global non-profit health organization, and, perhaps most bizarrely, in the late 90s during the upswing of her career, starred in *Anna Kournikova's Smash Court Tennis*, a critically acclaimed tennis video game for the original Playstation that pitted animated versions of WTA players against each other and other video game characters like Pac-Man. This kind of profile for a celebrity in a video game had not really happened before and would only really be surpassed by games like *Tony Hawk's Pro Skater* and sports simulations games like Madden, FIFA and PES.

Kournikova's public image and brand have outlived her actual tennis career. The perception never really goes beyond the realm of either her physical appearance or piss-taking about the disparity between her physical appearance and her skill (in Texas Hold 'Em, a type of poker game, for example, 'Anna Kournikova' is slang for a hand that includes an Ace and a King, not just because of the initials AK but also because the hand looks good but does not really play well). This is an unfortunate but natural side effect of employing such a marketing strategy—when people focus on looks, they do so to a fault. Regardless, the persistence is still there. I am not suggesting this as a viable avenue for young athletes; in fact, I think there are many moral issues to be raised about egging on such hyper-sexualization in a person who only spent the last four years of their career as a legal adult. Although this specific avenue takes courage and could be risky, the point I am trying to make is that parents are responsible for their children's strategy. Anna's example is worth mentioning for its effectiveness and ties to our more extensive conversation about an athlete's image. Her team achieved their goal—marketing her as an athlete with an identity outside of her gameplay which ensured her survival outside of the sport.

That is essentially what marketability is—a kind of long-term survival tactic. Every athlete needs to figure out how they and their legacy are going to survive off the court. This, like all fundamental aspects of elite athletics, is an ever-shifting reality, something that has to be worked and re-worked to fit each new phase of an athlete's life to both embrace and monitor change for a player's longevity. How a player fosters their image is ultimately up to them but it is our responsibility, as parents and coaches, to instil a sense of duty and awareness in athletes about the lasting effects of what is, ultimately, their most essential asset.

24

RESULTS

I have touched on a lot of different things in this book, everything from the pragmatic to the abstract, the financial to the philosophical. We have looked at different kinds of aspects of training, theory and industry, both in and out of the tennis world. For my own part, it is important for me to frame this knowledge with what is the most important aspect of making champions in any field or area of expertise. It is simultaneously one of the most talked about yet least understood elements of growth—results.

I am not talking about focussing only on wins or losses but rather about the idea that is at the core of any kind of athletic activity—the constant striving and stacking of various attempts atop one another in order to achieve greater success. When I talk about results, what I am really talking about is consequences—every action and every inaction, from the largest career move to the tiniest twitch of a muscle on the court, has a corresponding ripple effect. They need to be studied, understood and considered when moving forward, even the harshest failures. We can think about like a GPS—it is absurd to try and chart a path for ourselves without being honest about where we are and where that is in relation to where we want to be. We have to adjust accordingly, even when we get off track.

This book is called *How to Make Champions* for more reasons than just the clever play on words. It underscores a central point—the road to becoming a champion, especially in sports, is a process of accumulation or constant change and growth on every level. Every tip presented in the book and every aspect of training that we have discussed—everything comes together in the end. These things give you a series of slight edges and small advantages that gradually become bigger and amass to create an unstoppable force and help you reach miles ahead of your opponents.

Every Repetition helps you move forward. Every properly analysed loss moves you forward. Every opportunity, every endorsement and every point moves you further. Very rarely do athletes' lives hang in the balance of one outcome, one choice or one moment of devotion. In reality, this constant striving is like the tide, affected by a million factors, constantly ebbing and flowing, in and out and back in again. It is like the seasons, the natural peaks and valleys that come with time and development.

These metaphors are fairly cliché, as is the acknowledgement of their being clichéd, but none of that matters because, just like at the beginning of this book, I am urging you to look not past clichés but into them to see the sea of truth that lies in these old bromides. When you examine brass tacks, when you boil away all the pretence and posturing and all the pompous drive of the starry-eyed young and the projected wisdom of the veterans, what you are left with is one truth that is as simple as it is final—elite athleticism is all about playing the game because becoming a champion is a never-ending process.

Not only do I hope that you have learnt a lot from this book but also that you have learnt a lot about learning. I hope this book has helped you understand the complexity of lessons and the trials of communication so that you may, as a parent or a coach or as a curious athlete yourself, pass them on to the people you have sworn to support—your children, your students or even your own self. In addition, I hope that it has become clear how universal these principles are in so many ways and how applicable these ideas are to everyone, not just to athletes. I hope you have come to understand the nature of discipline in all its forms and what following the call of excellence can do for you.

EPILOGUE: ADVICE FROM VARIOUS EXPERTS

The road to becoming a champion, especially in sports, is a process of accumulation or constant change and growth at all levels. And in that process, you, as a parent, are critical.

The anecdotes and stories given below tell you more than a thousand words can.[25]

Sport is the children's career, not the parents.

—Hana Mandlíková,
former WTA No. 3

'I have two very talented children and I will tell you how I handled them. I'm sure I did similar things as my father did with me. He was an Olympic sprinter. When I was about 8 or 9, I wondered if I was fast enough to compete in the sprint. So when we went to the Spartak club, one of Prague's most prominent track and field clubs, we passed the oval track. Without hesitation, I said to Dad, "I'd like to try it." I didn't even have running shoes. "Can you take my time in a 100 meters?" I asked. "Okay," he replied. "Come on, let's try it." So I ran as fast as I could. I was out of breath

---

[25]All the anecdotes are taken from the author's personal interviews and interactions with the athletes and their family members.

and asked him, "Dad, how did I do?" "It was okay. Nothing special," he replied. "I think I'm going to play tennis," I said. My dad was my hero.

About five years later, when I had solidified my tennis career, my dad confessed that my time on the court had been good enough to have made me one of the top junior athletes in sprinting in the Czech Republic. See the idea behind that? He didn't want to push me to play the sport. He wanted me to play tennis. He didn't want to tell me I was good at track and field. This is what he told me: "Sprinting in tennis is not suitable for you. You have to know your kids. You can't force them to do something they don't want to do or don't feel in their heart. Yes. You have to guide them up to a certain age. Allow them, for example, to go to places where their friends go and do other things. But the point is, at 14 or 15, they should know what sport they love. Then you have to let them go and see. They have to want it for themselves. If you keep pushing and training them too much, it can be detrimental. When my kids were growing up, they were talented juniors but they got burned out. They played too much or felt too much pressure. They destroyed themselves mentally at a very young age. It has to be your decision to be a professional and good athlete. How do I stay motivated? I don't. I don't keep their motivations anymore. It's their life, their thing.'"

◆

Small rewards go a long way.

—Nicole Melichar-Martinez, former
WTA No. 9 in doubles

'If you have a talented athlete who wants to work, I think their parents have to give them more love and support, stand behind them and provide them with enough space. Because if your talented kid already wants to work hard, I don't think parents should try to push more. Parents should try to do their job as parents and make sure they're good kids who are respectful, say please and thank you and look their coaches in the eye when they talk to them. These are the core values that we can give our kids.

On the other hand, talented kids may need to be pushed a little bit more; but, at the same time, they should also enjoy practising. I think parents have to find a good balance of how to ask more of them without making them pressured. Sometimes, my mom would say, "Hey, if you win your game today, I'll take you to Starbucks; you can have a frappuccino." I feel like that little incentive was what motivated me to work hard. Giving a good reward if they do something well will help push kids a little more than saying, "If you don't do well, then I'm going to punish you."

My mom was the first person I hugged when I went up to the Royal Box after winning Wimbledon. My mom always came to my practices and never said much. She was always lovely. She would sit there with a smile on her face; and she enjoyed that her daughter was practising and playing tennis and had the opportunity to do something that she never had because she wanted to play tennis when she was young. But her parents wouldn't let her, so I think that's why she wasn't the typical tennis mom trying to train or get her to do too much. She would sit back and enjoy it because she saw that I was trying hard. She was living in the moment through me. I love it when she sees my workouts. I can see how proud she is of me, and I have to say the same thing about my dad. My dad always wants to help. It's in his nature. He wants to do it. He wants to feel like he can help me improve or maybe give feedback, whether it's to me or my coach. And he always has the best intentions, but sometimes I need to tell him to take a step back and enjoy a little bit more like my mom does. But I know his advice. My dad will always be the loudest voice to cheer me on in public. It's him against the stadium, and he beats them all. So I think I have the most fantastic tennis parents. I wouldn't trade them for anything.'

◆

The danger is when parents are coaches.

—Jimmy Arias, former ATP No. 5

'If I could give one piece of advice to parents of talented kids, it would be to make sure your kids are having fun in some way. Let them have a good time. It's not your responsibility to make their career.

I know it's hard for some parents. Some pros had a crazy parent behind them all the time and you know that usually that parent–child relationship has an ugly end.

But I think the players who have been more successful for longer had parents who wanted to give their kids opportunities but they didn't live vicariously through them. And a lot of tennis parents, I feel, lived through their kids in some ways; and it's more prevalent, I think, in tennis than in most sports because it's an individual sport. It's a one-on-one sport and there's no place to hide. When their son or daughter is playing, they are close to the court, watching and cheering them on. but sometimes they stray too far and their children get embarrassed. I think parents sometimes get too involved.

◆

*In my family, we have 2 world
number-one players.*

—Emilio Ángel Sánchez Vicario,
former world No. 1

'My parents belong to a typical tennis club. As a family, we often attended the club; we all went together and enjoyed different sports. For example, I played soccer and practised swimming by competing in small events.

I started playing tennis when I was eight; my sister also played and swam with me; we were about the same age. My two younger siblings also attended the club; they would show up carrying or dragging the racket. Our life revolved around the club; during the week, I was involved in soccer school but every weekend my parents were at the club all day. They loved playing tennis. We spent all that time playing and having fun with our friends in what I call 'the little battles', competing from a young age in mini tennis and different sports activities; it was a lot of fun, but we were just learning how to compete. Following our parents was our first step.

All those years at the club, playing and training, gave us the passion that took root; after a while, we started playing better and competing. My older sister went to train with the Federation, and later, I went too. When the Federation told me I wasn't good enough, the club helped me. Finally, at 14, I moved to a club with a better competitive environment. They helped me with certain costs, travel and other small expenses. The path is almost always the same—you start in a small club and when you improve, you decide to move to a better facility with better coaches to keep improving. Later, you move to a high-performance institution. This is the usual route for a high-performance athlete.

My sister and I were the best players in the world; it all started with our parents' core values. It was our choice to play tennis competitively, so our parents supported us, but in return, we had to be punctual, respectful of coaches and friends, work hard with 100 per cent energy at all times and never give up.

I have lived with this kind of discipline at home from a very young age. I lived that experience daily and made it part of my DNA.'

◆

If you're going to work with
your child, look for priorities.

—Robert Farah, former ATP No. 1 in doubles

'Smart parents play an essential role in developing their children to be their best.

But they must be careful because there is a fine line between pushing and pushing too hard. If parents push their children too hard, their children can get burned out;

and that ends up affecting the parents' relationship with the child. So they should use their intelligence and experience to know their children profoundly and have a direct way of handling them.

The best message I can give to parents is that time goes by fast; and parents have to take advantage of every minute, every hour, every month and every year that children are training. People progress very fast. If they want to get better, they have to get on the court with a purpose every day; that speeds up the process. Parents can guide their children by giving them small daily goals, so they have a clear plan when they practise.

Over time, children take responsibility for their practices. Prioritization is the most crucial part of a well-designed workout. What are we going to improve first? What exercises should I do? My father, Robert was my support system.'

◆

Let them succeed but let them be happy.

—Jim Courier, former ATP No. 1

'There are a lot of talented young people out there and my message to the parents of these athletes is to listen to them and be aware of what they are going through. I'm a parent. I have dreams for my kids. But I want them to pursue their dreams. And so I had a lovely experience with my parents. They encouraged my siblings and me to pursue the things we loved and were fully supportive of us. But they didn't pressure us. So we could follow our passions, not our parents' desires. And, from my experience, I think that's a good path.

I'm not suggesting that mine is the only correct path. There are other examples of parents who are a bit more energetic and their children are also successful in those endeavours. However, I can say with certainty that my parents' way promoted general happiness. I had a very happy childhood, which led me to continue to pursue something that I fell in love with early on and that I have never fallen out of love with, which is tennis. If you can find something that your kids stick to, support them and give them a push from time-to-time and guide them on the way forward. But if they pursue their dreams, they are more likely to be happy. And what more would you want for your children? Of course, we want them to succeed, but if they're miserable while achieving that success, I'm not sure that's a path I'd like my children to take.'

◆

It's vital to prioritize education.

—Nicolás Alejandro Massú Fried, former ATP No. 9

'My parents let me play a lot of sports. I think that's very important. I played rugby and soccer, and I did athletics. So, as a result, I was constantly developing. I loved playing sports and have always loved tennis and soccer. There was a time between the age of 10 and 11 when I was going twice a week to play soccer and four times a week to play tennis.

My first strong experience was travelling to play tennis. And things started to go well for me. I began to like individual sports a little bit more. So the advice I can give to parents is to make sure that their kids have a good time enjoying the sport. Let them develop on their own. Let them be the ones who ask you to take them to training, so they feel they are also committed. They are also leaders in the process. They also have to perform in school. Education is super important. Just because children are involved in sports should not mean they have to drop out of school at a very young age to play sports without doing anything else. That is a mistake.

You have to finish school first. Having an education is good for life. The advice is to let the parents play the role of parents, prioritizing education and letting the coaches teach the fundamentals and technical aspects of competition. Parents and coaches can make a great team, each taking care of their responsibilities and ensuring the child is happy and does well. The key is that the child shouldn't feel under pressure because if he feels pressured, he won't enjoy himself and won't want to play anymore.'

◆

It is imperative to teach values.

—Dave Fish, NCAA Museum
of Fame inductee, 2020

'I often talk about John McEnroe, but I'm sure he wouldn't have been able to play on my team because of his bad behaviour. Very different from Björn Borg, another superb player and a gentleman on the court, whose parents kept his racquets for 6 months because of his lousy on-court behaviour—he used to throw and break his rackets. People are willing to give too much license to talented players because they admire their skills. I had another young man whose name I don't want to mention. I forced him off the team because he treated people disrespectfully and terribly.

"Why do you think you've become that way?" I once asked him. "Well," he replied. "My parents don't care how I act as long as I win." And that, to me, is a sad story. And that's where parent and coaches have to set boundaries. Not to have rules but to let them know there's a safety barrier. And when you play within that barrier, life can be inspiring and fun.

But when you work in a company and break those rules, you're dishonest and that shadow will always be over your head. Things like cheating during a game, when the Ivy League college title is at stake, is wrong and goes against the values we teach.

Acting correctly at a young age and under pressure teaches athletes to make good decisions later. That's why some celebrities said it's easier to maintain integrity 100 per cent of the time than to figure out when and how to do it.

Parents should focus on the child's values and developmental goals. Competence is vital. But result-oriented parents can frustrate a child's development.'

◆

Parents sometimes get it wrong.

—Juan Carlos Osorio, father of María Camila
Osorio Serrano (WTA No. 33)

'The most important thing is that parents should always support their children. Help them in their commitments. When you take a child to a school or a court to play, you have to consider that the child enjoys the activity. Parents sometimes make a lot of mistakes. Why? Because it turns out that when we take our children to the courts for the first time, we enjoy them. But when the competition starts, we create pressure. No parent goes to school to pressure their child and tells them you have to do this or that. No parent stands at the school gate to watch the child. You have to let your child be and they have to enjoy those learning moments.

It should be the same in sports. We, as parents, are counsellors. Always talk to them positively. They are not always going to win. It's a long process. Regardless of whether the child does well or poorly, you should talk to them positively every time they have a dream. We have to help them; not to be the barrier in that process. Every time we talk to them or inform them of things, keep a positive attitude. We, parents, must be by their side to cultivate their dream positively. Their vision should become our vision. Be there for them in whatever they need. When the child is defeated, we have to support them; and when they are victorious, we do the same. For me, the fundamental thing is that parents never get to teach the sport. What we have to be is a support system. The coaches are the ones who direct the kids; sometimes, we parents get involved in things that are not our job. We have to be the fundamental support for the children so that they can achieve their dreams. I admire those parents who think about the process and understand the difference between being a parent and a coach.

The truth is that I have learnt, over the years, that the process results are more critical to María Camila's development. Parents cannot force the process forward. Everything in life has a process—the child first walks, then crawls, then walks, then runs. The same thing happens in sports.'

◆

It's a challenge to be a father and a coach.

—Andres Gómez, former World No. 1

'As a former player, I enjoy helping my son. The key is that this relationship does not become too stressful and that helps avoid compromising the father–son relationship. It is much more advisable to work with a select group of coaches, physical trainers, nutritionists, psychologists and tennis coaches and to trust them to make the right decisions.

Considering all the changes that occur in the career of a top athlete during their development, the team helps to improve performance and, more importantly, to maintain the relationship between parent and child. The most important goal is to keep that parent–child relationship. The parent should be the trusted figure that the child can lean on.

I'm not saying a parent can't or shouldn't work with their child, and I have done it too. I think there are ways to do it. I am saying that it is difficult for a son to work with his parents; we get too emotionally involved.

In any relationship in sports, the relationship between a player and his coach is always based on their chemistry.

Sometimes, it's essential to go beyond the desire to work hard; trust between the player, the parent and the coach is crucial. Everyone has to hit it off. The young athlete also needs close friends, someone to help him grow and a good influence off the court. All kids need friends and parents need to help them select the right relationships. Sometimes that person is not the parent; it may be the coach. As a parent, I help my son on and off the court; he knows he can rely on the parent, the coach and the friend. And I know I'm dealing with an elite athlete, a son and a friend. Raul is my best friend; and my son's coach and his close friend are a great combination.

Parenting and coaching intersect and it's not easy when things don't go well. So I had to find a way for us to be calmer during those difficult times. Finally, my son understands that I'm on his side, trying to contribute to his success and what he wants. He also knows that I'm always there for him.

He has fallen low and has been hit hard. During such times, it has been more challenging for me as a parent than for him and it's hard to hide those emotions. But, as difficult as it is, I have been very proud to be a part of his tennis life.

Tennis has evolved. There was a time when parents didn't interact with their children on the court. Jimmy Connors' mother, Gloria, was one of the first to be visibly involved. Chris Evert's father was too, but he was only seen at tournaments. Suddenly, we started to see many parents getting much more engaged in their children's development as athletes.

So much so, that a few years ago, there were a lot of known problems in the relationship between parents, coaches and their children. Today, that problem mostly stopped. I believe those fathers from the past opened the doors to the father–coaches of today.

Modern parents are very involved in their children's sports careers but are better prepared and more educated in the sport; they work with a team of trusted coaches. Parents want to see their children train and want to spend more quality time with them. Parents appreciate being able to give feedback and talk to the coaches and the kids. I strongly encourage parents to attend more coaching courses. I think there are many things we need to learn to be more effective parent–coaches. Parents need tennis knowledge to be effective guides, to know their child and the coaches better and think a little better about what they want to do as a team.'

◆

It's important to instil in them the culture of effort.

—Kumar Mehta, author of the bestseller
The Innovation Biome

'The most important advice I can give to parents of talented children is to create an environment where that talent can thrive. This encompasses two broad areas, with the first being the physical environment. At the most basic level, elite skill development requires easy access to facilities, equipment, coaching, mentoring and the ability to compete with talent and go head-to-head with others. Parents must ensure that these fundamental elements are easily accessible to their children.

The second area that parents must provide for is a psychosocial environment. Parents need to instil in their children a 'culture of effort'; this means that children grow up in an environment where excellence is always expected, not just desired. Children must grow up believing that outstanding achievement is within their reach and not reserved only for the stars or celebrities they see on television. In addition, children must understand the relationship between effort and results; in other words, they must realize that they have to work hard to achieve something. This 'culture of effort' is best instilled early in life and developing these skills in adulthood is challenging. Parents must do their part to create this environment for their children.'

◆

Everyone should attend college first
without losing their dreams.

—Leonard Roscoe Tanner, former world No. 4

'It's hard because I work. I keep fighting about what to do with my daughter because she's fast, mighty and can hit shots I can't believe. And as a parent, I walk a fine line between how much I should have her play in tournaments and how much I should have her train and learn to improve and love the game.

With the Williams sisters, Richard Williams made them very good before they played any tournaments. There's something to be said about that. But there's also something to be said about the toughness of the matches and the beatings. Let them learn from those defeats; it's okay to get beat. So we must put the sport in the proper perspective for these kids. We put a lot of pressure on young people and when you look at it, it's just a game.

I see parents uprooting themselves and moving elsewhere for their kids to play a sport. And often, they don't have jobs, so that kid naturally feels the pressure, knowing that the parents don't have jobs and now they're carrying the load. It's tough but that's the size of our game now. It's big and the stakes are gigantic. In some ways, I would love for the kids to have more fun with the game because it has to be fun deep down. But, unfortunately, there are lifetime sports and can open many doors to do other things. I wish kids would go to college because I think participating with a team is a great experience. Once you have a college degree, you're more protected because it's easy to get injured in professional sports. Then you don't have a college degree, so what do you do now that you're stuck? That's why I'd like to see young players gain maturity and experience from college. I recommend going somewhere with a good college programme and coach; some girls like Daniel Collins went to Virginia and had a good coach and now she's done pretty well on the pro tour. So I don't think college tennis keeps you from going pro.

Prize money has never gone down. It has always gone up. So if the prize money is continually going up, and most good pros play for about 10 years, you'll make more money if you take your 10 years later instead of earlier. So if you play 10 years later, it will be more money than today. I like that analogy.'